Advance

M000209423

COMMUNICATING POSSIBILITIES.
A BRIEF INTRODUCTION TO THE COORDINATED MANAGEMENT
OF MEANING (CMM)

Communicating Possibilities exemplifies what it means to live one's life in conversation—noticing details in moments of communication that matter and acting into them to enhance the chances of more desirable outcomes. The approach that Wasserman and Fisher-Yoshida articulate and demonstrate represents CMM's radical approach to communication in general and turn-taking in particular. Rather than focusing on the cues that enable smooth turn-taking, they argue for interjecting turns that make a difference. This is *turn-making* at its best."

> ~ *Arthur Jensen, Syracuse University*

The treatment of CMM offered by Wasserman and Fisher-Yoshida in *Communicating Possibilities* is one of, if not the, best short introductions now available. It provides a strong focus on what makes CMM a distinctive way to understand communication. Its examples are clear and I expect readily understood by students, teachers, and practitioners. I am particularly impressed by the way the authors have shown the connection between "cosmopolitan communication" and the other features of CMM theory. Given the present political situation that is surely an important contribution.

> ~ *Vernon Cronen, University of North Carolina;*
> *UMASS Amherst.*

This much-needed volume, *Communicating Possibilities*, provides an illuminating introduction to a ground-breaking theory of communication. Pearce and Cronen's ideas on the Coordinated Management of Meaning virtually transformed our conception of human communication. Most importantly, the ideas could be usefully applied to everyday life—in organizations, therapy, family exchanges, informal relations, and more. With new tools for reflection, new and more productive possibilities for action emerge, conflicts are reduced, collaboration encouraged, and creativity unleashed. With caring clarity, and rich illustration, Wasserman and Fisher-Yoshida provide an invaluable introduction to this fascinating domain.

> ~ *Kenneth J. Gergen, Swarthmore University; The*
> *Taos Institute and author of An Invitation to Social*
> *Construction*

This important book by Wasserman & Fisher-Yoshida provides useful examples and explanations of some of the essential features of CMM, such as a systemic understanding of patterns of communication, multiple contextual constructions of meaning, and a framework for mapping out complex processes of social interaction to make changes or open new possibilities. Especially effective is the emphasis Wasserman & Fisher-Yoshida place on sequential and reflexive unfolding of meaning and action. In light of the challenges we face in these times, such a heuristic communication model is especially needed, one that considers the social construction of ethics, different forms of awareness, and patterns of communication that we create together. This introduction to CMM provides valuable resources and tools that facilitate an ongoing conversation filled with new possibilities.

~ Victoria Chen, San Francisco State University

Communicating Possibilities is an inspiring book about how to use CMM in the various contexts of our lives—from our most intimate relationships to the larger systems of which we are a part. Wasserman and Fisher-Yoshida provide relevant and useful examples that help the reader see how to use CMM mindfully and compassionately in all aspects of our social worlds. This book is a "must read" for anyone interested in living intentionally and compassionately in our complex and divided world.

~ Kim Pearce, Founder and President, CMM Institute
for Human and Social Evolution

Dear Mark, & Judi
I so treasure getting to know
you both - serving with you, Mark
to the possibilities you & we will
create...
together
love, Ilene

Communicating
Possibilities

*A Brief Introduction to the Coordinated
Management of Meaning (CMM)*

Ilene C. Wasserman &
Beth Fisher-Yoshida

Taos Institute Publications
Chagrin Falls, Ohio
USA

COMMUNICATING POSSIBILITIES
A Brief Introduction to the Coordinated
Management of Meaning (CMM)

Copyright © 2017 Taos Institute Publications
© 2017 Ilene C. Wasserman & Beth Fisher-Yoshida

Cover and Design Layout: Debbi Stocco

Taos Institute Publications
A Division of the Taos Institute
Chagrin Falls, Ohio
USA

ISBN-13: 978-1-938552-54-0   LCCN: 2017936189

Printed in the USA and in the UK

Introduction to
Taos Institute Publications

The Taos Institute is a nonprofit organization dedicated to the development
of social constructionist theory and practice for purposes of world benefit.
Constructionist theory and practice locate the source of meaning, value, and action
in communicative relations among people. Our major investment is in fostering
relational processes that can enhance the welfare of people and the world in which
they live. Taos Institute Publications offers contributions to cutting-edge theory and
practice in social construction. Our books are designed for scholars, practitioners,
students, and the openly curious public. The **Focus Book Series** provides brief
introductions and overviews that illuminate theories, concepts, and useful
practices. The **Tempo Book Series** is especially dedicated to the general public
and to practitioners. The **Books for Professionals Series** provides in-depth works
that focus on recent developments in theory and practice. **WorldShare Books** is an
online offering of books in PDF format for free download from our website. Our
books are particularly relevant to social scientists and to practitioners concerned
with individual, family, organizational, community, and societal change.

— Kenneth J. Gergen
President, Board of Directors
The Taos Institute

For information about the Taos Institute and social constructionism visit:
www.taosinstitute.net

FOREWORD

MY ACADEMIC CAREER WAS LAUNCHED at the heels of the Coordinated Management of Meaning. From 1978 until 1982, I had the good fortune to study and work with Barnett Pearce and Vernon Cronen. Those were exciting years, marked by the blossoming of Barnett's idea of coordinating how we manage our meanings into an elaborate theory and method for the study of human interaction. There was a great intellectual fervor brewing in the halls of the Department of Communication at the University of Massachusetts in those days. Graduate students, along with Pearce and Cronen, would gather on weekends, as well as weekdays and nights, to brainstorm applications, methods, and concepts to further elaborate CMM. Barnett referred to our marathon sessions as the "CMM Sweatshop." We were all honored to be assisting in the evolution of CMM!

In those early days, we were playing with the idea of a hierarchy of meaning—a hierarchy that had the potential to be fluid and shifting as interaction unfolded. We also were concerned with mapping the act-by-act emergence of an interactive pattern. We explored strange and charmed loops where the recursive nature of meaning and action could be mapped, as well as logical force, which helped us examine the degree of obligation one feels to act in a certain way. We designed studies to test these tools and to explore how they assisted our understanding of human interaction, the "stuck-ness" of some interactive patterns, and to point out the potential avenues for transformation.

It's important to add that at the basis of CMM has always been an interpretive, pragmatic approach to the study of human interaction. Since the reigning tradition in 1970s and 1980s social sciences was (and to a great degree still is) empiricist, those of us working within the CMM perspective often were not taken seriously at national and international conferences. Respondents wanted to know where the "evidence" was.

Designing methods for mapping logical force, hierarchical contexts, and recursivity gave the CMM group a place at the table of (more or less traditional) social science. In retrospect, we could even say that it took CMM into an entirely different realm; it provided complex mapping techniques that, while quite useful for those skilled in their operation, left many others perplexed. With so many models and so many terms, to many, CMM was just too complex to grasp. It's interesting to reflect now on how adding complexity to CMM brought respect and acknowledgement from the broader academic community, while taking it further away from practitioners for whom these ideas should have been most useful. This reflection highlights the unfortunate chasm between the scholarly world of academia and the pragmatic world of professional practice.

Since those early days, CMM has evolved and shifted. Rather than focus on providing evidence of how an unwanted pattern of interaction persists, CMM has emerged as a set of resources for looking at communication as opposed to through it (Pearce, 2007). Barnett called this "taking a communication perspective on social worlds" (p. 53) and summarized it in the following four questions:

- What are we making together?
- How are we making it?
- What are we becoming as we make this?
- How can we make better social worlds? (p. 53)

The present volume is an illustration of both the return to the original pragmatic, interpretive roots of CMM and its expansive evolution. In this long-awaited volume, Wasserman and Fisher-Yoshida provide the first articulation of the Coordinated Management of Meaning designed as a guide and resource for both practitioners and academics. They present a clear, descriptive introduction to CMM and illustrate, with vivid examples, how the CMM tools for noticing and naming communication patterns can help interacting parties attend to "critical moments," thereby transforming unwanted interactions into more desirable patterns. As mentioned, central to CMM is the idea of "looking at" communication rather than "through it." To that end, CMM offers several resources, each of which Wasserman and Fisher-Yoshida describe within the ongoing process of noticing-observing-reflecting-engaging-noticing (again); they use the acronym NOREN. The authors have structured their book around these phases of "noticing" which move in a reflective spiral of unending curiosity.

In short, CMM resources equip practitioners and scholars with the means for attending to the moment-by-moment flow of actions that coordinate to form both desirable and undesirable interactions. If we can change the patterns that emerge from these moment-by-moment coordinations, we can change our relationships. CMM takes "a communication perspective" and in so doing, moves us away from psychologized explanations and understandings of social interaction, replacing psychologized "mental states" with what people do together—interaction—thereby allowing us to see what sorts of life-worlds our doings create. Communicating Possibilities will be a much read and much used book.

Sheila McNamee, PhD

University of New Hampshire; Vice President, the Taos Institute

TABLE OF CONTENTS

FIGURES

INTRODUCTION

INTERACTING WITH OTHERS on a daily basis and making sense of these encounters is becoming increasingly challenging. News spreads quickly and new information redefines what we thought we knew. No sooner than when we reach a decision with our work team, do we get a strategy-changing memo. We are still reading and responding to a news cycle on one topic when the next story that is taking the media by storm appears and often redefines the first story with significant consequences. On many occasions, we walk away from a conversation wondering what just happened.

Reema, one of our clients, an anesthesiologist with a 25-year tenure in a hospital practice, shared such an experience:

> I entered the room for our weekly team meeting. I came straight from another meeting and, unbeknownst to me, someone had brought a television set into the room for the group to watch the news of a terrible bomb blast—a terrorist attack in Paris. I was wearing my hijab that day. When I walked into the room, all eyes turned toward me. It felt like the friendships I had built over 10 years of working together

dissipated and suddenly I was a stranger… it was as if I had become "one of them" in their eyes. Since I had not yet seen the news, I had no idea why there was a shift in how people responded to me.

In the course of any day, in any moment, any one of us may experience something that causes us to become confused. Up until a particular moment, things seem to be going along quite smoothly, and then, suddenly, a shift happens. It could be a moment where we feel tension or disconnection with another. It could be something someone says—or doesn't say. It could be an email intended or not (i.e., sent by mistake). Sometimes these moments pass quickly and sometimes they linger, perhaps triggering a deeper sense of mistrust. These interactions are known as *speech acts*, in which an exchange occurred between people in the process of communicating.

There are many examples of these sorts of narratives that may become polarized and that exist on personal, ethnic, and political levels. We may know someone who is feeling the pain of estrangement from family members due to deeply rooted stories of misunderstandings and insults. We may ourselves have experienced the loss of a significant relationship—a friend, a romantic partner, a position at work or in the community—because something went off track. Sometimes we think we know what happened or at least have a reasonable seeming explanation; at other times, we just wonder in uncertainty. In many places, wars are being fought, people are being displaced, and populations are being destroyed because of deeply held narratives with strong moral judgments of right- and wrong-doing.

This book is about the ways in which we shape our lives through the stories we create in our ongoing conversations. Collectively, they become our social worlds. In the process of taking a step back and looking at our communication and how we construct our social worlds, we open up the possibilities of alternative paths and subsequent outcomes. This exploration of different perspectives can lead us to consider how we respond, which in turn leads us to becoming more intentional in

> *This book is about the ways in which we shape our lives through the stories we create in our ongoing conversations.*

how we engage others. This intentional engagement can transform our social worlds into better places.

Introducing *Coordinated Management of Meaning* (CMM)[1] is one method to help achieve those better worlds. CMM extends the traditional view of communication beyond a message transmitted from sender to receiver to the relational process of meaning making together. In the transmission model, we craft a message and hope or expect the receiving party to understand it the way we intended. However, all too often, this is not the case. In the CMM model of communication, there is a back and forth process between parties that creates a rhythm and shapes meaning making. Sometimes the rhythm feels like a smooth flow—almost melodious. Sometimes the back and forth feels stilted and abrupt. Still other times, there is the sense of a premature ending or a questionable closure. In any case, the back and forth processes are always invitations or imperatives to respond—in some way. Before we know it, meanings are made and/or shifted, and our socially defined worlds are being made. As such, communication is both *"something"* in and of itself and a process that is *consequential*[2]. We say it is consequential because every communication has an outcome and this influence, strong or weak, shapes our understanding and our next interaction. Communication IS consequential.

3

When we take a step back to observe the interactions instead of being caught up in them, we can better see the patterns we are creating. Each back and forth between communicating parties can be thought of as a "turn." The collection of turns makes the pattern of the communication. CMM offers a way of looking at the patterns we create and identifying the ways in which those patterns shape our relationships. Seeing the patterns from different perspectives and frames enables us to connect in a different way. As a result, we may understand the situation differently, which might lead us to change our response at the next turn. This is where we have the greatest potential to transform the quality of our relationships.

Seeing the patterns from different perspectives and frames enables us to connect in a different way.

Consider this simple example: You are busy at work. You try your best to be responsive to your friends and family, but find yourself in an undesirable pattern of complaint and defend—others complain and you defend. Noticing this back and forth pattern opens up new possibilities and paths going forward. Just naming and framing this pattern is one step, i.e., "I notice that…" Noticing provides openings to shift the pattern from disregard to empathy and consideration.

We make patterns together. We are relational beings in webs created by being together. Gergen offers that we are relational beings, "the whole that is equal to the sum of relations."[3] As relational beings, our new and expanded understanding of patterns offers us more nuanced ways to respond. These new responses, in turn, influence the nature of our communication and relationship, and these new behaviors enable us to sustain the changes these transformations bring.

This book articulates some of the key concepts of the Coordinated

Management of Meaning (CMM) and what it means—from a relational perspective—to develop as people together in conversation. We illustrate these conceptual frameworks with stories from both our professional and personal lives to better demonstrate the points we are making. We also use a variety of illustrations from the concepts and models of CMM to visually depict the stories we are describing[4]. These visuals highlight different elements of CMM and the multiple perspectives that are possible. Our desire is to meet you where you are whether you are a practitioner, a student, a life-long learner, or any combination of the above, by looping stories, concepts, and visuals throughout the book. We do this as an attempt to build comfort in engaging with this process, regardless of the level of familiarity you may have with communication theory or CMM.

As a result of reading this book you will learn:

- How to shift from *being in* your story to stepping back and *looking at* your story;

- Tools for noticing and naming the patterns you create in relationship with others;

- Ways to notice the deeply embedded triggers that create undesirable repetitive patterns of communication;

- Strategies for creating new patterns and better social worlds and futures.

And... this is a journey.

The genesis of this book was an invitation to bring a simple interpretation of CMM to the world of practitioners as well as students of communication. We, Ilene and Beth, were introduced by Barnett Pearce, one of the first authors of CMM. We both studied with Barnett while pursuing our doctorates at the Fielding Graduate

5

University. Our engagement and connection with CMM was imme-
diate. Over time, our conversations with Barnett took many turns
and we enjoyed (and still do) the discovery of new ways of seeing
and making sense of our worlds through the lens of CMM. One of
the aspects that impressed us most about Barnett was his openness
and curiosity to continue the conversation of developing CMM. He
genuinely appreciated the turns others took in growing CMM and the
interface with other perspectives

CMM continues to provide us with a framework for being active, intentional and mindful agents of our lives and relationships.
they introduced and grew in
relationship. We were fortunate
to join that conversation. CMM
continues to provide us with a
framework for being active, intentional and mindful agents of our
lives and relationships.

This book is the first of what we hope will be a series of CMM
Focus Books published by the Taos Institute. This volume is an
introduction to CMM concepts and practices. Future Focus Books
will elaborate on different topics taking a CMM perspective. Already,
CMM and Research Methods is in press.

We hope you will join us in the ongoing conversations about
making better social worlds across contexts using the CMM communication perspective.

CHAPTER 1: CMM—COORDINATING AND MANAGING MEANING

THERE ARE THOSE OCCASIONAL MOMENTS when we think we understand the social norms, and then something happens that doesn't quite make sense. We begin with a story of an encounter between three women—Teresa, Sara, and Mary, who are anticipating having lunch to debrief a very important meeting, and the staff of the private club where they made a reservation. They are early and the lunch crowd has not yet arrived.

1. Hostess: Feel free to sit wherever you would like.

2. The three women choose a table by the window and sit down. They are very energized by the meeting they just left and are eager to debrief. The waiter brings them menus and water. A few minutes later, the waiter returns with another person, both looking concerned.

3. Waiter: I am so sorry but I am going to have to ask you to move. Women are not allowed to sit at this table.

4. Sara: You must be kidding.

5. Waiter: I am afraid I am not. This table belongs to the Foxes and Hounds and they don't allow women.

6. Sara: We just came from a meeting of the most senior women in the city. And you mean to tell me that we cannot sit here because we are women?

7. Waiter: Yes.

8. Sara: Would you give us a minute?

Sara, a new member of this club is appalled. If she were to pause, take a step back, and notice what is influencing her reaction, she might identify a few issues: First, she is a successful professional woman and is shocked to learn about the rules of exclusivity in this club she just joined. She also is concerned about her guests. This next turn in the conversation is what we identify as a "critical moment.[5]" Using CMM tools and frameworks as lenses through which to understand and make meaning from this encounter, Sara would be able to see the many layers of influences and perspectives shaping this interaction. This would provide her with multiple ways of framing the incident and allow her to gain access to the different ways those who are directly and indirectly involved may see and understand it. She would be able to consider how any choice she may make in this or other critical moments is consequential and creates the next turns in the engagement. In addition, the ways others in this interaction respond influences the communication and together they co-create the meaning making process.

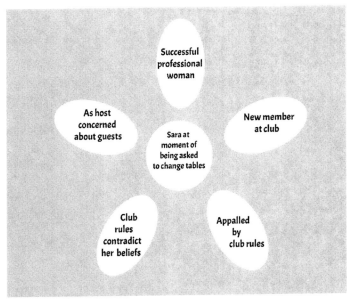

Figure One: CMM Daisy Model to explore factors influencing Sara's decision making

CMM takes the standpoint that communication is central in making social worlds. Communication is not only about the end result, but also about the process, the path we take in moving towards these outcomes. We make or shape our relationships in every interaction we have. Every turn in our conversation is a choice even though at times we are not aware of making choices. These choice points have the potential to take us down different paths, which lead to other choice points and our choices are consequential.

In the vignette above, the first three turns may be framed by the social formality of an invitation—an episode of hosting. The women were colleagues, they were debriefing the first meeting they had convened as a team, and they were anticipating the continuation of their collaboration. The fourth turn may be considered a request or a confrontation. The meaning of the situation is not inherent in the words alone. Rather the meaning of that situation is further contextualized by the interchange(s) that preceded it and the subsequent responses that will occur as a result of it.

Communication, in the form of words and actions, explicit or implicit, creates complex and complicated webs of relationships. These webs of relationship make our social worlds. Some meetings, such as between a manager and subordinate or professor and student, have a historical or formal structure that enacts a power relationship. Those titles create deeply embedded patterns of roles that have an inherent force that has developed over time and shapes the dynamics even before the first utterances. Performance reviews and exams, which we can refer to as "episodes," also have forces of their own. These can include expectations and norms regarding who initiates, who responds, and how each is enacted. Marriage, and the expectations and attributes associated with it, defines a future path of a relationship and—in many situations—rights and privileges. Words have a way of defining lived realities within a social context before the interaction even begins. This activates historical hierarchies, organizational charts, policy manuals, authority dynamics, privileges, expectations, and more.

CMM highlights the patterns we create in the process of trying to coordinate our actions with each other and managing/making meaning in the process.

CMM highlights the patterns we create in the process of trying to coordinate our actions with each other and managing/making meaning in the process. As social beings, we do not operate in isolation; we live in interaction with others. We try to understand our encounters while we are in relationships with others. We are simultaneously in the midst of the communication and, perhaps, also trying to take a step back to notice the patterns we are co-creating. There is interplay between the way we *manage* our internal awareness, the *coherence* (or the stories each of us tell about what is happening) we strive to reach with our interpersonal exchanges, and *coordination* of *meaning* making (what we do together); this is how the name CMM—the coordinated management of meaning was derived.

Questions, such as "what are we making together," "how did that get made," and "how can we make it—our social worlds—better?" are central in CMM theory and practice. These questions lead us to shift from focusing on intentions—which locks us into analyses of individuals and their cognitive processes—to focusing on relational processes. Tracing the flow of our interactions (the turns) and identifying the patterns that led us to our current point of communication allow us to identify possible responses to these questions. The different turns in our conversational exchanges are opportunities for directing the conversation's path. In other words, we can act with a stronger sense of agency and awareness because we are making deliberate, rather than habitual, choices. The shift from individual analysis of intentions to analysis of the ongoing relational processes presents huge opportunities.

In referring back to the story of the three women in the restaurant, the moment the situation changed from an open invitation of "sit wherever you want" to the statement that "you are going to have to move" was critical. Sara seemed to be taken by surprise that she was being asked to switch tables. She continued probing because she was experiencing dissonance between the experience she and the other women had earlier that day in a meeting of senior executive women, to what she perceived as a diminishing of her status by the waiter in the club restaurant. The waiter continued to clarify his request with

11

a rational explanation. Sara asked for some time to confer with her colleagues and could use this as an opportunity to take a step back and disengage emotionally from that interaction.

One way to interpret and make meaning of this situation is to consider the context. We operate within multiple contexts at any given moment. We do not always realize or focus on these multiple contexts, yet they exist and surface when we pay attention to them. Until the critical moment, the highest context for the women and the hostess was mutual and coherent: an open invitation to sit anywhere. The third turn, when they were asked to move because women cannot sit at that table, shifted the highest context from invitation to imposition, as a rule, previously unknown to the women, superseded the open invitation. This shift of context from being welcome to sit anywhere to an existing, but unknown, rule being imposed was a critical moment. The women had many ways in which to respond, but might not have realized it and therefore reacted in their default mode. Their next turn may follow the shift and result in changing their table; or it could have been a turn by the waiter to make an accommodation and allow them to remain; it could just as likely have been confrontational; or some other possibility. Sara's request for a minute to consider her response allowed the women to think through their options and the potential consequences. More often than not, we don't take the opportunity to pause and therefore end up in situations that could have been avoided if we had taken the time to consider what our next turn could be and the potential impact of that choice.

The communication perspective

CMM subscribes to what has been called *the communication perspective*. The core principles of the communication perspective are:

- **Communication is substantial and performative: It does something.** Communication creates the quality of our relationships, our social worlds. If we step back and look at, name, and frame the patterns we create in the ongoing process of communicating, we can be more intentional in our "performance" of helping make better relationships and social worlds.

- **Communication is consequential.** Every decision we make about how to actively communicate, or not communicate, is fateful. How we engage others leads to outcomes in the form of their response. We react to these responses, which then influences the next turn and the cycle continues. We create feelings, attitudes, and action with each choice we make. This continuous back and forth flow creates patterns in our relationships with others. Some patterns are destructive, some constructive; some we want to sustain, others we want to change.

- If we **transform our patterns** of communicating, we can better transform our relationships. Considering and anticipating the patterns and trajectory our conversations are producing helps make us aware of choices that can alter destructive patterns. The positive outcomes of more desirable conversational flows energize us to continue creating more constructive patterns.

Communication can be thought of as a reflexive cycle in which *actions create meanings and meanings, in turn, shape actions.* We can take a communication perspective by looking at this interactional process reflexively.[6] Social worlds are

Communication can be thought of as a reflexive cycle in which actions create meanings and meanings, in turn, shape actions.

made of interconnections amongst the selves, relationships, organizations, communities, and cultures that we create *in and with communication.* The social worlds we create also shape us.[7] A conversation between persons "does something to them quite apart from the issue they are discussing."[8] The act of reflecting on our communication patterns provides opportunities for more coordinated meaning making with others; while we are actively engaged in the communication itself, we also step back to consider the communication. Rather than consciously or habitually resorting to default responses that may hamper our relationships, we can be more intentional and use every exchange to learn about and/or improve relationships.

In the restaurant scenario, Sara's moment of pause allowed her and her colleagues to consider different options and conversational interactions they could create. Reema, who felt something different in her relationships with her co-workers when she walked into a room of colleagues watching the news, might have fallen back to a default reaction of silence and withdrawal; an alternative could have been to pause and ask a reflective question, such as: "What just happened?"

"The stories we tell may differ from the stories we live."[9] We are continuously making up stories as a way of making sense of our lives. Yet our stories are always unfolding in the context and intersection of others' actions and reactions and the stories they are making.

The three core principles of CMM are coordination, coherence, and mystery. We are *coordinating* with others in the turn-by-turn relational processes of our communication. At the same time, we strive for internal *coherence*—an alignment of our meaning making processes with the unfolding interaction. And, in all of our interactions in our social worlds, we are continuously managing a sense of the unknown, a sense of *mystery.*

The patterns we create consist of a series of turning points that are the choices we make during our interactions with others. Each choice has a consequence and sets the stage for the next interaction. Some choices are more significant than others because they have a stronger influence on our relationships; these are critical moments. All interactions have an afterlife, but critical moments have a bigger impact and longer afterlife. They influence significant shifts in our interactions and lives. For example, if Sara's next turn was to call her good friend who anchors the local news to encourage her to do a media blitz of the sexist practices of the restaurant, she would be setting in motion a much different afterlife than, for example, talking privately to the owner of the restaurant or moving to a different table with her friends. All patterns have unknown aspects and once articulated, influence how we understand the process.

Patterns have forces of their own. If we seek to change the nature of one of our relationships, one choice or action has the potential to start the ball rolling. However, to permanently change an already established pattern, one shift may not be enough. Subsequent turns to support these changes will be required. Transformation is an ongoing process of multiple turns, not an individual event.

In the next turn of our restaurant story, Sara begins to weigh her options and solicit feedback from her colleagues:

9. Sara: I think we have three options: One: stay where we are. Two: change tables, but ask to speak with the general manager. Three: just leave. What do you think?

10. Teresa: I can't believe they have this rule. I think we should just stay here and wait for the general manager.

11. Mary: We could also leave.

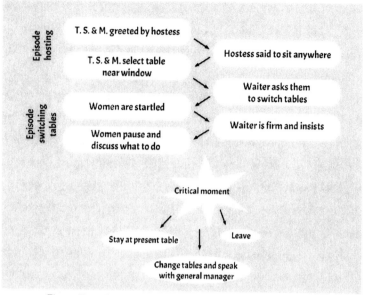

Figure Two: Representation of Club Restaurant scene using Serpentine Model, critical moments, and episode markers

At that moment, the waiter returned with the restaurant manager.

a. Restaurant Manager: I am very sorry, but the person who offered you this table did not realize that it was the Fox and Hounds' table. She should not have seated you here. We can lose our jobs for this.

b. Sara: Really?

c. Restaurant Manager: Yes. The Fox and Hounds is a private club within the club and they do not admit women members. If the President of the club sees you sitting at this table, he can have us fired.

This is additional information to the women. They now realize that their decision in the next turn could have serious consequences for the staff of the restaurant. This information engenders a potential shift in their attitudes and influences their available choices.

As stated earlier, transformation is an ongoing process, as is the meaning making that accompanies it. The subsequent turns in conversations expose new information and influence the range of choices available to us as the process continues, potentially changing our frames of reference.

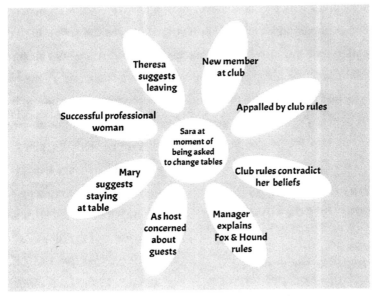

Figure Three: Enhanced CMM Daisy Model with input from Sara, her friends, and the manager

Our frames of reference are created by the experiences we have and the meaning we create from those experiences. The new piece of information about the threat to the staff's job security shifts the context of the conversation once again and influences how Sara and her colleagues will respond. Prior to learning this new piece of information, Sara's colleagues were considering whether to challenge an exclusive rule that seemed to contradict the club's commitment to inclusion. As they talked about what to do, the potential impact of their choice to stay at the table in protest was superseded by the potential consequence that others might lose their jobs. The additional information created a new context and shifted what informed their deliberation in this context.

In each turn, we see new considerations for framing the experienced episodes. We create these frames by considering contexts and determining which contexts take the highest place and influence all other contexts and frames. The stories we create through communication and the turn-by-turn processes unfold in twists and turns; sometimes unpredictably. The story emerges as new aspects are told, heard, and felt. Taking a third-person perspective of our communication patterns allows us to step back and witness the communication flow and to make changes that lead to our desired outcomes. In stepping back, we can look at the relationships we are creating and determine whether they align with what we want. If the relationships do not align, then we can adjust our actions for the next moment, or turn, we take to create our desired outcome. Seeing the options for creating new possibilities and using our own agency to make them happen is empowering.

We use the acronym NOREN as a way to think about the reflective cycle: Notice; Observe; Reflect; Engage; Notice again, repeating the cycle in a spiral of perpetual reflective learning.

There are many patterns of stories. Some stories we live with in resonance and others in dissonance. Contextual forces, or the sense of obligation that we feel to respond in certain ways, influence them all. Throughout this book, we explore these forces through examples of episodes of interaction, including, but not limited to, the contexts of family, friendship, business, travel, and governance. Each context creates and perpetuates influences, such as the role of identity, power, integrity and emotions.

We use the acronym NOREN as a way to think about the reflective cycle: *N*otice; *O*bserve; *R*eflect; *E*ngage; *N*otice again, repeating the cycle in a spiral of perpetual reflective learning. The word NOREN refers to traditional Japanese fabric dividers typically hung in doorways, between rooms, on walls, or in windows. Their main purpose was protection from dust and dirt. NOREN separates one space from another as a metaphor for the reflective cycle. The process of noticing, observing, reflecting, engaging, and noticing again is similar to stepping out of the room you are in and returning moments later with a new perspective.

We have many examples in our everyday life where we have gadgets or gestures that shift, limit, or expand our frame of meaning from filters on our mobile phone cameras to editing functions on photo apps that narrow and focus the frame of what we are seeing. We also have examples of zeroing in on one or two of our senses (closing our eyes to smell better; holding our nose and closing our eyes to elevate the sense of taste). Think about the NOREN process, and the tools we describe, as ways of highlighting how we make meaning of our social worlds, and as invitations to open up possibilities.

In this chapter, we highlighted the following principles and concepts:

> It is important to take a step back to reflect before acting.

> Coherence exists in our internal awareness and coordination exists in our interpersonal exchanges.

> The importance of identifying critical moments and the potential consequences of our choices.

> Episodes are how we frame situations or interactions and the meaning of these episodes are co-created in relationship, in context.

➤ Episodes contain Logical Forces that strongly influence meaning making AND provide for any shifts in context.

➤ The turn taking we do in conversations has the potential to transform meaning making.

➤ CMM helps us look at coordination, coherence and mystery as part of our relational processes.

In the next chapter, we look at the process of Noticing, the first *N* in the acronym *NOREN*.

CHAPTER 2: NOTICING (NOREN)

HAVE YOU EVER HAD THE SENSE that you were missing something during communication? That information is presented, but the logic is not clear, or something is missing from the sequence of events, or the choices someone made may seem odd and you feel that if you could see more clearly, or know the full story, you could better understand and navigate the moment better? In this chapter, we highlight what is involved with "noticing" during the communication process. The communication perspective places an emphasis on looking at and noticing what is produced in the interactions people create in their communication. Let's talk about what it means to notice.

In our opening story, when Reema entered the lunchroom, she was intuitively reading or sensing something in the room—before she could even attach words to it. All too often, we are observing and shaping a story before we notice that we are doing it. The human characteristic of meaning making distinguishes us from other living organisms; we need to explain and understand what is taking place because we need to know how we will be affected by it. Perhaps this links back to our innate survival mechanisms in that we need to know whether we are safe or in danger. This need to ascertain our safety probably started with a focus on threats to our physical safety.

When we step back and take a third-person perspective, we are able to notice patterns in our communication. Noticing is the first step in developing awareness. To notice and identify patterns we create in our meaning making processes, we need to take a meta-perspective. This implies that we are creating some cognitive and emotional distance between being in the interaction and observing or noticing what is taking place. The old adage "can't see the forest for the trees" makes sense in that when we are in the middle of the forest, we notice individual trees rather than seeing patterns of the forest made by the trees. Taking a step back, creating distance, allows us to separate ourselves from what we are in the midst of and notice. Shifting from being immersed in the dynamics of an interaction, to the third party meta-perspective of *looking at* the dynamics from a distance allows us to see communication patterns.

> *When we step back and take a third-person perspective, we are able to notice patterns in our communication. Noticing is the first step in developing awareness.*

Here is an interaction between co-workers that can help illustrate these points.

Joanna and Jeremy were working on a project together—or so Jeremy thought. Jeremy was taking the lead in preparing the presentation and was relying on Joanna to coordinate with him on her progress. Joanna contacted Jeremy and this interaction unfolded:

1. Joanna: I just came from a meeting with Rosemary (the sponsor of the project). She is really happy about our progress and looks forward to our presentation.

2. Jeremy: I thought we were working on this together!

3. Joanna: Of course we are. I just happened to be in a different meeting with Rosemary and took the opportunity to check in with her.

Is this pattern familiar?

Joanna thinks she is being collaborative. Jeremy's response is potentially confrontational. Once we notice and begin tracking and understanding the patterns we create in our interactions, we can better view the relationship and anticipate the outcomes and consequences fostered by the patterns. Jeremy and Joanna are noticing that something happened; something that is shifting their commitment from collaborating to questioning their collaboration, all within one turn of their conversational flow. In this case, their noticing from a meta-perspective opens up the opportunities to check the outcomes and consequences of their coordination. Their reactions to one another differed from their intentions and now there is a chance to mindfully realign their coordination in the next turn of their conversation. How Joanna responds during her next turn is consequential.

From the communication perspective, any number of turns can be grouped into what we refer to as an "episode." This specific interaction between Jeremy and Joanna can be framed as an episode, as can the total period of time Joanna and Jeremy have been working together. The interaction between Joanna and Rosemary can also be framed as an episode. An episode is based on the scope of the interactions, or turns, on which we want to focus. Let's consider the different episodes that may be made by the responses or turns Joanna can offer as she continues this interaction with Jeremy:

If she says: "Why are you being so sensitive?" What does she make in this interaction or episode?

If she says: "Ahhh. I can understand you're feeling out of the loop. I had to make a decision in the moment. We were just finishing our other meeting, and she asked me for a briefing on how we were doing. Why don't I give you more details about our meeting and see what you think?" What does she make in this interaction or episode?

Joanna's turn sets the stage for Jeremy's next turn and so on in their interaction. Taking a meta-perspective and noticing the patterns within which our interactions with others occur provides the space for us to shift our perspective and realign to our intentions in the communication. If Joanna and Jeremy both take a step back, they will be able to see how they each interpreted, or made meaning of, one turn very differently and how this difference in interpretation could potentially jeopardize their collaboration. New information was being shared and thus opportunities for new meanings to be made that could advance or destroy their relationship depending on their shared and respective histories were created. If Joanna had asked the first question we posed, it could trigger a defensive response or even an expression of vulnerability from Jeremy.

1a. Joanna: Why are you being so sensitive?

2a. Jeremy: I just finished a project with George and he totally ran over me in the process. I felt like my contribution was invisible and it affected my performance review. I was so relieved to be working with you on this project. I trusted that it would be different with you based on how we have worked together in the past. Your meeting with Rosemary triggered a question about whether I could actually trust you!

Until this conversation, Joanna did not know about Jeremy's previous work experiences with George and how sensitive he was to working collaboratively and being able to trust his colleague. Upon

24

hearing this, Joanna took a step back and considered her interaction with Rosemary from Jeremy's perspective. While her intention was to advance their work together, she now sees Jeremy's perspective— that this was a step toward creating a rupture in their collaboration.

Resonance and dissonance

We experience a rhythm of resonance and dissonance in the process of shifting perspectives and making new meaning. The dissonance comes about because we are processing new information that potentially shifts our perspectives out of our familiar comfort zones and from realizing that our interactions may not be moving according to our intentions of how we wanted them to develop.

Let's see what happens if Joanna instead responds to the pause noted above and makes an observation (rather than ask a question) in the next turn:

1b. Joanna: My intention was to share information with Rosemary on our behalf. I'm wondering if I did something to offend our collaboration.

(This is a choice point. There are many directions this episode can go depending on Jeremy's response. One is to make an episode of hurt and insult as in the example below.)

2b. Jeremy: I thought we were collaborating. By having your own conversation with Rosemary you are making it YOUR project not OURS!

(or…Jeremy could respond by joining in the episode of observation.)

2c. Jeremy: I realize I was assuming that you would contact me to join your conversation when the opportunity arose. I wish I could have been there to support and add to the conversation.

The episode Joanna and Jeremy are making together continues to be defined by Joanna's next response and the back and forth exchanges or turns between the two of them. Again, this might take multiple forms.

Consider the different episodes each of these responses potentially "makes":

3a. Joanna: Jeremy, it is difficult enough to find time to work on this project! Coordinating our every move is yet another challenge!

(or....)

3b. Joanna: Ahhh. That is helpful. I can see how you would feel that way. I also can understand how—had you been there—your perspective, being so close to the presentation, would have made the conversation all the more productive.

(or)

3c. Joanna: I am sorry. I know you are particularly sensitive to being included in the ongoing conversations. I will make sure to consider that more closely in the future.

In this last turn, Joanna creates an episode of empathy and elevates a more specific and explicit commitment to the collaboration. It is more personal than the other possible responses we explored.

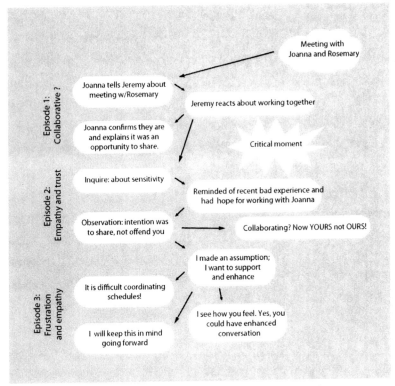

Figure Four: Flow of conversation and possible turns using
Serpentine Model, critical moments, and episode markers

If the outcomes of our back and forth communication exchanges do not go as expected, we may ask ourselves, "What just happened?" Sometimes it is subtle while other times it can be a very strong sensation. When this happens, we are interrupting our previous patterns of communication and creating new ones. This is because we are challenging the assumptions that were guiding our interaction. However, creating new patterns is not easy. To do so, we need to go through the process of NOREN: Noticing, Observing, Reflecting, Engaging, Noticing again. NOREN with specific action steps can be: becoming aware (noticing), stepping back (observing), identifying choices (reflecting), being mindful of what we are creating together (engaging), and then starting the iterative cycle again (noticing again).

In addition to coordinating our meaning making with others, we strive for internal coherence. States of dissonance take us further from coherence and we work to return to the comfort of familiarity and predictability. This means we may hold to communication patterns and meaning-making processes that do not serve us well in our relationships because they are familiar and comfortable. In Jer-

> *... creating new patterns is not easy. To do so, we need to go through the process of NOREN: Noticing, Observing, Reflecting, Engaging, Noticing again.*

emy's case, he has had experiences with competitive and mistrustful colleagues. While he may not like this pattern of deceit, he has learned to protect himself from it and function within it. His collaboration with Joanna offered him an opportunity to grow because his experiences with her to this point led him to believe she was trustworthy and not competitive. However, trusting her and letting down his guard would require him to suspend assumptions that have led to the habits he has formed for engaging colleagues. His previous experiences have led him to develop certain ways of knowing; suspending these habits would lead him to experiment with the ambiguity brought on by *not knowing*. This new type of encounter is a mystery at this point and the initial discomfort will become comfortable once it is familiar. To suspend habits and engage mystery, we need to trust the process. As this becomes embedded in our frames of reference, we may encounter new experiences that lead to a new wave of dissonance, and so the cycle continues. The concept of mystery is an underlying principle of CMM as we learn ways to cope with the unknown.

Feelings of resonance come about after periods of dissonance.

When we have resonance we are in sync with others; our meaning making is coordinated and all feels good. The more positive our experience when moving between resonance and dissonance, the more fluid this movement becomes and the more we trust in the process and ourselves, the more expansive our new communication patterns become. We may also develop new levels of comfort with ambiguity or mystery and our threshold for coherence becomes higher.

Throughout this book, we offer conceptual frameworks as tools for looking at what we are doing and making together; tools that strengthen our reflective muscles. Here, we articulate four forms of communicating. Each form possesses unique characteristics and reflects different views of self, other, and relationship.

Forms of communicating

We have a natural capacity to differentiate "us" from "them" in relationships with others. One manner of noticing is comparing ourselves to others by wondering "Are you the same as me?" This is a developmental skill that begins at a very young age. We can observe this in children when they notice simple things like "You and I have the same color shirt." or "You and I both have a brother." We also notice this when groups of people form clubs, clans, or other types of affinity groups. We have multiple aspects of who we are and how we identify ourselves. When we compare ourselves to another person, we foreground a particular part of our culture or identity, i.e., race, ethnicity, nationality, tribe, gender, or affiliation, so that we are either similar or different on that point of comparison. Pearce[10] identified four forms of relating: *monocultural, ethnocentric, modernistic,* and *cosmopolitan.* Each of these forms has communication patterns that are typical to it. Depending on the context, we may engage in more than one form of relating; when the context shifts, it's possible that the form of communication shifts as well.

Monocultural communication refers to the form of relating when we notice only the aspects of others that are like us and do not notice those aspects that are not like us. This is because we are not able to see difference; it literally implies that we act on our beliefs that there is only one culture. By treating others as though they are just like us, regardless of differences between us, the unique qualities of others are not valued and they may feel invisible. However, we are unlikely to be aware of their feelings because we expect them to also be monocultural (like us). One example of this is to suggest that "we are all alike" or that "you are just like me." Such a claim is more likely to be made by someone who, in part, defines or is representative of the dominant culture. They would view such a statement as an inclusive gesture. One of the appeals of monocultural communication is that it rarely presses us beyond relaxed thinking; differences are neither expected nor encountered.

Ethnocentric communication refers to the form of relating when we begin to differentiate between them and us. It means we recognize there is a difference, and we view the other culture from our own culture's perspective. This sets up a dichotomy. In ethnocentric communication, distinctions are made between *our* stories and practices as differentiated from *their* stories and practices. We are likely to view these differences with a great deal of judgment and those who are different are not valued as highly as those who are similar. Distinctions are made from the perspective that 'our' views, beliefs, and practices are the 'right' ones and yours are wrong. There is no room for divergent opinions, beliefs or values.

Modernistic communication values change. The highest value

30

is placed on progress and the way forward—bigger, better, faster. Differences are tolerated as long as they do not impede progress. Paradoxically, traditional beliefs are devalued as outdated and inhibiting the progress narrative. When viewing the world from this form of communication, we are always looking for the next new big thing. Because change is good, personal identity and self-worth derive from making changes; the modern communicator sets out to make changes. This value on the "what's next" can create "casualties" for those who are "left behind." It can also create instability in any long-term relationship or project. There is a hesitancy and reluctance to impose one's own thoughts at the risk of offending others. In these instances, we may say nothing or go around the issue rather than confronting them head on.

Cosmopolitan communication refers to the form of communication where the inclination and the capacity to notice differences and be curious about them exists. It is not like monocultural communication, where we might not notice difference; nor is it like the ethnocentric form where we might be fearful and judge difference against our own norms and practices. Instead, cosmopolitan communication is a form of relating that enacts a commitment to coordinating meaning making with others, beyond just progress and change, by appreciating both similarities and differences—including both the other's unique existence or humanity and ours. It acknowledges and allows the space for different types of beings to coexist in relationship to each other in the same world.

The key distinction among the four forms of relating is the extent to which we hear and recognize the existence of stories, which may differ from our own, regarding the way things should be. There are degrees of willingness, tolerance, and acceptance of parallel stories of the human condition. Monocultural, ethnocentric, and modernistic forms of communication are each governed by the characteristics of their own meta-narrative, from which notions of values, morals, and beliefs are judged. Cosmopolitan communication, on the other hand, holds that many narratives can coexist simultaneously with many more nuances of values, morals, and beliefs without the need for one over-arching, governing meta-narrative. This is a significant differentiation.

Moving from monocultural to cosmopolitan communication requires increasing our willingness to see that other stories of existence hold value. This can be an unsettling proposition if we are deeply committed to our own stories and fearful of alternative perspectives. This willingness to allow for the existence of other narratives requires a capacity for managing complexity and being able to hold multiple narratives side-by-side with our own.

> *Moving from monocultural to cosmopolitan communication requires increasing our willingness to see that other stories of existence hold value.*

Consider the complexity of how these forms manifest in our encounters. In one instance, as women, we might distinguish ourselves from some patterns of masculine culture and therefore take issue with the utterance: "I don't see women as different from men; I treat you all the same." Yet, as white women, we might perpetuate the same pattern when amongst a group of women from multiple cultural backgrounds and assert that we are all the same. In both instances we would be speaking from the perspective of the dominant culture in that setting or context. Each of us may be similar to others in some ways and different in other ways. The cosmopolitan form of communication anticipates and explores the complexity of variations with differing levels of similarity.

In one of our earlier examples, Reema walked into the room for the team meeting and she saw herself as a valued and contributing member of the team, supported by years of history. Yet, in a micro-moment, she encountered a contradiction to that narrative; a narrative in which she was *different* or a *suspicious other.* For Reema, this was unsettling and likely disorienting. It was a shock to be cast into a role she had neither anticipated nor desired. As well practiced as we might be in engaging others with the form of cosmopolitan communication, one turn, one event, one prompt of fear and mistrust, can shift our form of engaging.

Capacity for complexity

As we said at the beginning of this book, daily conversations are becoming more challenging, especially with competing worldviews about the way the world should be. Inevitably, our perspectives and subsequent judgments change as more information is added to the storyline. Martin Buber[11], an Austrian-born Israeli philosopher known for his work on dialogue and the quality of relationships, spoke of the "fully human way" as the path to go forth into the possibilities of relationship. This requires a willingness or openness to risk our sense of individuality in the presence of the relationship. There exists a balance in the tension between holding our own beliefs and values while being open to and accepting of the beliefs and values of others at the same time.

Kegan[12] saw adult development as a process of engaging the tension between separating and differentiating from others and the desire for connecting. Each developmental stage of Kegan's initial model is a way of addressing the lifelong tension between the yearnings for inclusion and distinctness at the same time.[13]

33

As we develop, we often realize that we are *in over our heads*[14] and need a road map, a guide, or curriculum to help us navigate the complexities of everyday life. Adult development involves an increasing capacity for complexity. Cosmopolitan communication describes a capacity for holding multiple perspectives at the same time and to do so in a way that helps us observe what is unfolding. Amidst the complexity is a sense of mystery brought about by not being fully aware of all that is involved. As new information becomes available to us, new twists and turns in our meaning making processes continuously unfold. Robert Kegan's stage theory[15] for adult development posits orders of logic through which we evolve and develop an increasing capacity to consider and integrate new experiences into the stories we narrate.

The first orders of logic are primarily those of child development, with the first being the orientation toward learning about the world. In this stage, the world is viewed as always changing, thus there is no sense of constancy. Consequently, the child likely requires reminders about rules and expectations. In the second order, the person recognizes constancy, and can attend to concrete tasks and rules of social engagement. Choices are concrete lacking nuance and are made in relationship to weighing rewards and punishment.

Adult development is typified by the latter three orders[16]: the socialized or interpersonal stage, the self-authoring stage, and self-transforming stage. The process of adult development is described by the increasing capacity individuals have to know themselves as both separate from and related to the social world around them. When we exhibit the third order of consciousness, defined by Kegan as the socialized stage, we are more connected to others around us, are capable of nurturing mutually enhancing relationships, and are very much influenced by them. We define ourselves in relationship with others which, at times, intensifies the tension between differentiating and connecting.[17]

In the fourth order of consciousness, we are more self-initiating, self-correcting, and self-evaluating. People in this order of consciousness "have the capacity to take responsibility for and ownership of their internal authority"[18] and establish their own sets of values and principles. Relationships become a part of one's world rather than the reason for one's existence. We are initiating a stronger sense of agency in the way we assert ourselves in the world.

The interdependent self builds on this in the fifth order, enacting a world that allows for simultaneous belief and acceptance of contradictory or incommensurate views. We can manage the complexity and mystery of life better than at any of the other levels of development. At this order of knowing, we regard the self in context of other relationships; perspectives we hold are seen as incomplete and multilayered, needing others to be fully constructed. The contexts of others contain additional information that influences what we notice and how we make meaning of our relationships.

According to Kegan, most people are able to recognize that there are different forms of thought and that these can create challenges among people. The challenge is that often people are not able to look at their own system of thinking as but one form and that, without a capacity for trans-systems thinking, people cannot see the limits of their own worldview. They are, therefore, less likely to be able to create new forms of engaging that synthesize otherwise incommensurate realities.

The tools and frameworks of CMM support taking a third party perspective that enables us to "have our story," rather than, as Kegan suggests, "be had by our story." This is an important distinction. The ability to take a third-person perspective and look at a situation, or our story, enhances our capacity for complexity—a necessary competency in today's world.

Episode framing

To this point, we have referred to social encounters as interactions consisting of moments or speech acts, and turns. In our story of Joanna, Jeremy and Rosemary, we used the term "episode." In this section we highlight and expand the notion of episode framing. Paying attention to the naming and framing of an episode helps us look at situations from alternative perspectives. This expands the possibilities of information, meaning making, and action in relationship with others. For example, we recently facilitated a meeting during which one of the participants felt frustrated with the process they were experiencing. It went something like this:

1. Paul: I think it is time for us to discuss the design of the team meeting.

2. Warren: I don't see how we can talk about the design of the team meeting when we don't have clear authority about the strategy we are taking. I have been patient with this conversation up until now. But it is clear that we cannot talk about design until we know our strategy!

3. Paul: But we only have one hour left in the meeting and we need to come away from this meeting with a design.

4. Warren: We need to come away from this meeting with a sense of how we are running the business.

Is this a familiar pattern to you? If Paul and Warren were to stay in the current back and forth pattern, continuing taking these types of turns, we might see them become increasingly entrenched and frustrated with each other. They are likely to feel that the argument is becoming personal.

As the facilitator, we assumed the perspective of the observer, or a third party.

5. Facilitator: I think it would be helpful to look at this conversation through the perspective of episode framing. For example, as I have been listening, for you Paul, this meeting has been an episode of planning a workshop. For you, Warren, this has been an episode of strengthening the business model. Is that the way you both see it? Let's pause for a moment and determine how we want to proceed.

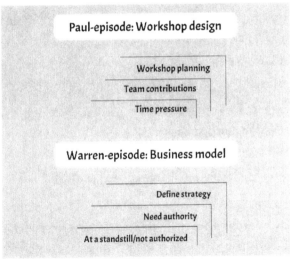

Figure Five: Different levels of importance in framing the purpose of the meeting using the Hierarchy Model

The CMM Hierarchy Model[19] is designed to help us look at the contexts within which we live and our stories of life exist, how the contexts influence our decision-making processes and actions, and how the contexts shift in priority and influence with each subsequent turn.

The third party observer, the facilitator, takes a step back and is able to see the two different ways in which Paul and Warren were framing this episode. How they frame the meeting determines their behaviors, communication, and expectations. This, in turn, leads them to either feel the meeting was successful if their expectations were met or was a failure if it flowed as a differently framed episode. Surfacing these implicit assumptions and expectations is a way to draw clarity and repurpose the episode to align expectations. Naming and framing the episode in relationship with transparency allows the alignment to take place.

In this chapter, we highlighted the following:

➢ The acronym NOREN highlights noticing, observing, reflecting, engaging and noticing again.

➢ Noticing communication patterns from a third person perspective is a first step in developing awareness.

➢ We introduced Kegan's orders of logic in adult development to describe the increasing capacity for observing oneself in relationship.

➢ An episode consists of a series of turns in conversation.

➢ In the process of relating with others, we sometimes move between resonance and dissonance, between understanding and not understanding. Mystery is the experience of not understanding.

➢ There are four forms of communicating: monocultural, ethnocentric, modernistic and cosmopolitan. They differ in *how* the perspective of the other is considered.

> Dialogic communication is the process of holding the tension between having your own perspective, while being open to the other.

> The Hierarchy Model looks at the stories within each context and how that influences our decision-making.

CHAPTER 3: OBSERVING
Framing and Reframing (NOREN)

*Ultimately, CMM is a way of thinking about our-
selves. Its ultimate questions are "who are we?"
and "how shall we live?" (Barnett Pearce)*

IN THE COURSE OF ANY GIVEN DAY, we deal with various types
of complexity that influence how we make meaning of our lives,
our interactions with others, and how we choose to act in the next
moment—even if these are not conscious processes. We make meaning of each moment based on a variety of factors, such as how we
prioritize the contexts in which we are involved and the stories we
tell and are told about those contexts. A context can be home, our
role in our family, our work, a political rally, school, and so on. Some
moments in these stories, which are embedded in contexts, seem
more critical than others.

In this chapter, we focus on the aspect of observing by taking a
third-person perspective on the moments we create as we participate
in them. We, and other CMM practitioners and researchers, have
found that the tools and frameworks of CMM provide an anchor
point of sorts to hold ourselves to an observing stance, while at the
same time being and engaging. In the episode with Joanna and Jeremy, when Joanna was sharing the conversation from her meeting

with Rosemary we see, using frameworks and models, what they are making together by highlighting how the process of coordinating meaning is continuously shifting and turning. The better we can "see" that, the more adept we can be at choosing how we co-create the next moment.

The forces that influence meaning

While presenting at a conference, Elizabeth approached a thought leader in her field, Ed, about the possibility of reviewing and commenting on a book she was writing. Initially, he responded that he would be happy to meet with her and suggested he'd be in touch.

The following day, they ran into each other and Ed shared that he was feeling overwhelmed and anxious by the crowds at the conference and was ready to go home. He offered the possibility that they share a car service to his home city (a six-hour drive). He did not want to deal with changing flights and getting to the airport and realized that the drive might be a simpler alternative. Further, he did not want to arrange for the car service and suggested that if she wanted to make the arrangements and drive with him, they could use that time to talk about the book.

Consider how this invitation unfolded from Elizabeth's perspective:

"At first, I felt intimidated. Until that point, Ed had been one of the key scholars/authors who had informed my work and the field as a whole. I was contextualizing this episode by elevating rank, stature, and evaluation. Another consideration was that I had made a commitment to helping another elderly colleague, Richard, get to the airport and wanted to make sure he had an alternative if I were to leave the conference early. Yet another consideration was logistical: Accepting this invitation would mean leaving the conference early, canceling other commitments I had scheduled, giving up my flight for a six-hour drive and then arranging for an additional six hours of travel home.

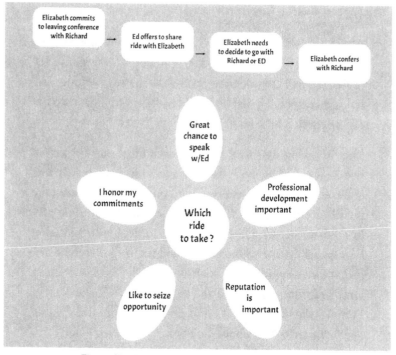

Figure Six: Elizabeth uses a Daisy Model to explore influences in her decision making flow

"When I spoke with my colleague, Richard, he said without pause, 'First, you don't have to worry about me. I can make other arrangements to get to the airport. Second, what a great opportunity to spend time talking with Ed. Think of it as making a new friend.' He also shared some additional context about some personal changes that Ed was going through. The conversation with Richard shifted the episode from an engagement of rank and hierarchy to a more relational, human encounter.

"Even before I had this conversation with Richard, I realized that I had all these preconceived notions about Ed. With this additional piece of context, I shifted my attention from rank and evaluation to just enjoying the time with Ed."

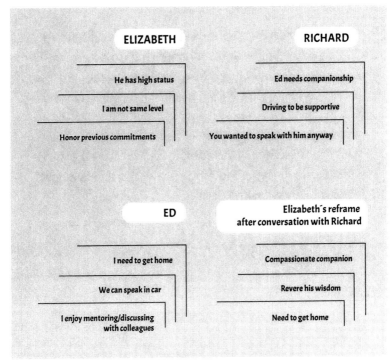

Figure Seven: Shifting perspectives of relationship in context using Hierarchy Model

What did they make? When we come together with others or choose to remain alone, we make our relationships and social worlds. The shift from naming this car ride as an evaluation or assessment to naming it an opportunity of creating a friendship, reframed the episode from, in some respects, objectifying Ed to being present as one human being to another. That shift enabled a mutuality in the

43

conversation that would not have been present before this shift in framing. As Elizabeth tells the story:

> "From the moment we started the ride, the rhythm of our conversation was one of exploring ideas followed by standing back to notice what we were making. We were attending to each other, and I was present to him and what we were creating together.
>
> "We have since enjoyed several visits; each with no specific agenda. Each visit is an opportunity to be present to each other and to explore what we learn in that process. This opportunity to privilege 'just being together' is noticeably unique. In western culture, we often tend to privilege a tactical goal or purpose when coming together with others. With Ed, attending to what is important to each other in the particular moment in our lives, our relationship and, making shared meaning, is primary."

In the first turns of a request and a suggestion, a new episode emerges. Each turn opens the potential to expand or constrain a relationship or lead to a dead end. In this case, a collegial relationship has continued to unfold, influenced by a new foundation—an unusual opportunity of six hours of emergent dialogue.

Another example of framing and reframing episodes involves two colleagues, Karen and Halima, in which Karen faces a choice that has competing considerations. Karen met Halima at a professional conference more than 10 years ago. Despite residing on different continents, they stayed in touch and built their friendship while seeking ways to collaborate. Recently, Karen was attending a conference close to Halima's home. Both were particularly excited about the opportunity to see each other and reconnect with their shared professional interests: building bridges that connect people from different ethnic groups, particularly those with a history of mistrust. The only opportunity for Karen to visit Halima would be on her way to the airport. Karen's hosts expressed concern about her plan and were concerned that taking a taxi from Halima's town might arouse suspicion and subject Karen to a delay when she arrived at the airport.

The choice of how and when to visit Halima, and how to travel to the airport, was a *critical moment* for Karen. We mentioned earlier that some episodes we experience are more complex and more critical; this was one for Karen. In this moment, multiple contexts were influencing her decision-making process:

- The local stories about social and ethnic identities told by her hosts, stories about *safety and security*,
- Her *relationship with* and *trust with* Halima,
- Her *relationship with* and *trust with* her hosts,
- Her *story of self*—who she is and how she acts, makes choices, and so on.

Each context has a story of what 'should' be and what choices she 'should' make. There are moral elements to the stories we tell and live.

As we consider Karen's dilemma, let's revisit the concept that meaning is continuously emerging and being reshaped in conversations and in how we name and frame episodes. Here, we add the consideration that episodes include multiple contexts (i.e., the actual episode, one's story of oneself, the importance of the relationship, the cultural stories, stories of safety, stories of encounters with differences and cultural constraints, etc.).

Let's look at the multiple contexts we use to create and shape meaning.

45

Karen's social world:

Story of self: Trusting, caring, curious

Story of (these) group(s): Mistrust and adversarial

Relationship: Mutually supportive and trustworthy with Halima; honoring the care and advice of her hosts

Episode: Building relationship; getting closer; more personal

Context: Making arrangements to visit Halima

Culture: Mistrust; not safe

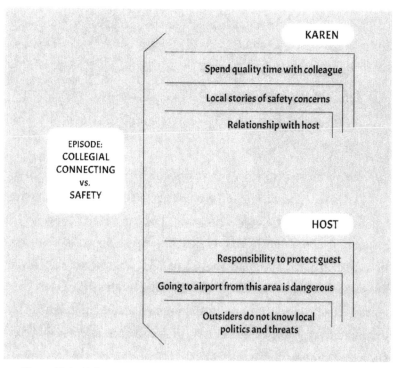

KAREN

Spend quality time with colleague

Local stories of safety concerns

Relationship with host

EPISODE:
COLLEGIAL
CONNECTING
vs.
SAFETY

HOST

Responsibility to protect guest

Going to airport from this area is dangerous

Outsiders do not know local politics and threats

Figure Eight: Differing perspectives of importance and relationships in context

When two or more participants see, understand, and articulate quite different stories about a situation, there are implications for how they frame the episode. For example, in this particular situation, relationship is Karen's highest context. The second highest order of context that informs her choice is her story of self as trusting and curious. Karen's desire to be trusting and curious was in tension with the advice she was getting to be careful. The advice to be careful was in conflict with her sense of safety and security, which is influenced by the conditions of the town where she lives in the United States. The contextual forces for these decisions in her hometown is quite different from the forces that inform decisions made by Halima and the individuals who were giving her advice.

Framing perspective

The vantage point from which we see the world influences how we perceive and understand—name and frame—the world around us. When we take a first-person perspective, we cannot see communication patterns because we are the center of what we create. We are central to and embedded in the dynamics we are co-creating with others and are emotionally engaged in what is taking place. It is challenging for us to take a different perspective or to see things unfold any differently than what we are experiencing. Yet when we take a step back and distance ourselves from the dynamics of the communication, we take a third-person perspective and view the situation objectively with us as the subject. This stance allows us to create more distance and be more emotionally detached from the situation and, at the same time, more empathic to what is being made. It enables us to notice patterns of communication we may not have previously noticed because we are viewing them from a different perch.

47

We make decisions and enact communication patterns with the data we have available to us in the moment. This data is likely to be limited and partial, taken at a particular point in time from a particular perspective. Given the complexity in the world, we are unlikely to have the full story or any substantial amount of data that creates any communicative interaction. It may seem as though we are entering midstream into an episode or a conversation that started before we entered and will continue after we leave. We are but one part of a multi-turn conversation. The more limited the data set from which we reference information, the more narrowly focused and limited our understanding. The stance we take influences how we interpret information and make meaning. Our position in relation to the communication (subjective or objective) causes us to notice things differently. This, in turn, introduces different sets of lenses that we use as filters through which to make meaning. An analogy in the past would have been how sheets of velum added to an initial picture, changes, or enhances what we see. Now, we have the example of apps on our mobile devices that add color and other effects to a photo we take—thus changing the very scene we just captured.

The question is: To what degree are we aware that we are working with a limited data set? The more conscious we are of the limitations of our understanding, the more open we can be to raising questions that provide an opening to gather more data, shift perspective as appropriate, and re-order the contexts of our Hierarchy Model.

CMM provides an entry point that enables us to unpack the inferences we make. It encourages us to ask a different set of questions to frame the conversation in a way it would not have been framed had we not asked those questions. Shifting our perspective and asking questions from that alternative perspective aids us in uncovering our assumptions. We base our decisions and actions on the inferences we draw; when we uncover our implicit assumptions, we are able to make more informed decisions.

In the episode we were describing, as Karen was considering when to meet with Halima and how to coordinate her meeting with traveling to the airport, multiple forces were influencing each other. Looking at these contexts and the forces within them helped Karen notice the patterns being made, the subtle rules that were making those patterns, and how those forces and rules created choices. While Karen can try to consider the various contexts on her own, she recognized the benefit of seeking the perspectives of a third party to help her identify and expand how she named the complexities of the different contexts and influences. The CMM communication perspective provides the tools and frameworks for stepping back and looking at the patterns made, how we created them, and the choices we elevated so we can be more intentional in making future choices.

Another model Karen found helpful in choosing what to do in this episode is the LUUUUTT Model. LUUUUTT is an acronym for 1) stories Lived; 2) Unknown stories, 3) Untold stories, 4) Unheard stories, 5) Untellable stories; 6) stories Told, and 7) storyTelling.

This model helps unpack complicated and complex stories. It can be used to explore the gaps between the lived and told stories, stories that are more vocal and those that are muted, stories that are under-developed or silent, and the manner in which the stories are being told. The model is used to enrich and expand the layers of stories we and others tell, broadening and deepening the episode and meaning making.

What stories were being told about how taxis from Halima's town are treated when they arrive at the airport? What were the unknown stories about travel in this part of the world? What are the untellable stories about how ethnic tensions influence relationships among the different groups?

Moving from inner dialogue to interpersonal engagement

The capacity for complexity is stretched when we are engaged in these critical moments and have to both sort out the various influences and potential impacts and, at the same time, make choices about how to go on together. All too often, the amount of time we need to sort out the complexity is much greater than the timeframe available before we need to act. How do those involved distinguish what is best as inner dialogue? When and how does engaging with the other enhance the quality of what they are doing and making together?

Paul and Warren, introduced in Chapter Two, who were discussing the team meeting, were able to move beyond the back and forth pattern that had trapped them in the past and to step back together to discuss the purpose of the meeting once they framed the episode. They were able to deepen the conversation with sharing, on a more personal level, their disappointments with the organization in the past and the emotions that were tied to this critical juncture.

Episode framing helps us look at the continuous process of meaning making by separating an otherwise continuously evolving episode into a temporal sequence of beginning, middle, and end to help frame a storyline.

The Serpentine Model highlights the flow of events, interactions, and turns of what is said and done between and among people.

The Serpentine Model highlights the flow of events, interactions, and turns of what is said and done between and among people. At each turn, there is a "critical moment", a "pivot point[20]", or a "bifurcation point" that is a choice point. Each turn presents an opportunity, a choice to take any number of directions. We have been looking at these turns in terms of the types of episodes these turns create. The moment of dissonance with Joanna and Jeremy had the potential to shift when we looked at the turn that framed competition and mistrust as an episode of efficiency and collaboration. Looking at the Serpentine Model, we can see how considering the episode in the context of future turns better supports that shift. How are the turns they create today going to influence their future turns? To this point, Jeremy's work experiences have included episodes of both collaboration and disruption. His experiences with disruption had greater impact, thus his pattern was to more easily move to mistrust. Episode 1 (See Figure Nine) is punctuated by Jeremy's response:

Jeremy: I thought we were collaborating. By having your own conversation with Rosemary you are making it YOUR project not OURS!

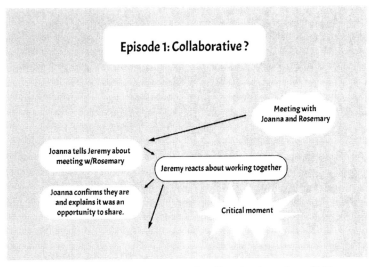

Figure Nine: Jeremy's response to Joanna's telling about meeting with Rosemary

Episode 2 represents what might be created if Jeremy chose a different response; a response that takes into account his pattern of mistrust, yet shifts his relationship to the pattern from being the subject of the story to being an observer of the story. The observer perspective presents other possibilities of storytelling.

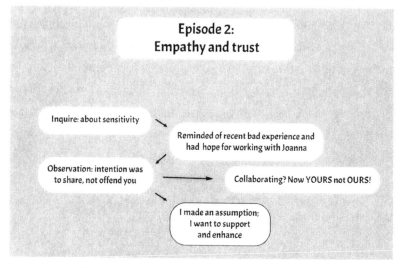

Figure Ten: Alternate potential response from Jeremy

Joanna, on the other hand, has an inclination toward openness. By choosing to look at the episode together, they were more apt to move into a future of mutual trust and collaboration. Consider Joanna's possible responses in the making of Episode 3:

> Joanna: Ahhh. That is helpful. I can see how you would feel that way. I also can understand how—had you been there—your perspective, being so close to the presentation, would have made the conversation all the more productive.
> or
>
> Joanna: I am sorry. I know you are particularly sensitive to being included in the ongoing conversations. I will make sure to consider that more closely in the future.

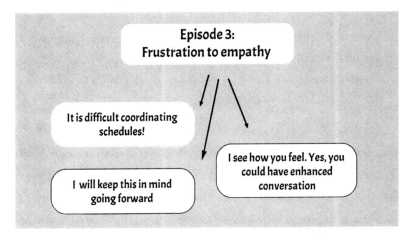

Figure Eleven: Joanna considering alternative responses to Jeremy

All too often, our responses have a force of their own. "He says this, so I have to say that—I have no other choice." The Serpentine Model helps people look at how these forces of habit can be choices and how, by looking at the choices we are making, we can choose different paths.

Thus far, we have looked at episodes that are primarily associated with the workplace. When we share this model with our clients, they inevitably share stories of how it has helped them with their personal relationships. One spoke of how helpful he found these frameworks and tools when applied to issues between him and his wife. In the next section, we introduce some examples outside the work context.

The forces that influence meaning

You're sitting in traffic. The light turns green and the car in front of you doesn't move. On another day, you might be more patient, but today you are late for an important meeting. You feel compelled to honk your horn.

Or... Fill in the blank with any example you can think of where you feel compelled to respond in some way—to perform a pattern that seems to have a history long before you entered the story and will continue to have a force of its own once you have exited.

Logical force is the sense of "oughtness"—that propels what we do, what we should do in *this* episode or *this* relationship at *this* time. These forces are developed by our history, such as cultural and personal experiences, family, education, and societal influences. Logical forces are recursive; they help us create new stories that align and are coherent with the stories of our past (i.e., I have to honk because I am late for a meeting and I value being on time).

Logical forces can take several different forms—*prefigurative, practical, contextual* and *implicative,* for example[21]. With prefigurative force, we add our "turn" to a previously shaped conversation to build on something that has already happened. We do so to affirm our story of how it should be. Practical force is when people act to initiate something that aligns with their hopes and expectations. Contextual force reinforces how people like us have a given type of conversation in a given context. Implicative force describes how the result of an episode is connected and consequential to the next episode. In some ways, it prefigures the next episode and reshapes contextual forces. We build on these definitions with examples in the next chapter.

In this chapter, we highlighted the following:

➤ The Hierarchy Model shows the multiple contexts existing simultaneously that influence meaning making.

➤ The contexts change positions in the hierarchy and meaning is influenced by the context we elevate as our priority.

> Each turn in the conversation has the opportunity to transform meaning.

> We make our assumptions explicit by shifting perspective and asking questions.

> The LUUUUTT Model unpacks the multiple stories coexisting that makes communication complicated and complex.

> There are stories in each level of context and they have their own logical forces of what should and should not be.

> There are four types of Logical Forces: prefigurative, practical, contextual and implicative. Each influences the meaning-making process in different ways.

> The Serpentine Model highlights the flow of events, interactions and turns within and between episodes. Each turn in the Serpentine Model is a critical moment where we have choice about how to respond.

> Episode framing creates meaning by identifying beginning, middle and end.

CHAPTER 4: REFLECTING
Ethics and Moral Choices (NOREN)

THE EXAMPLES WE HAVE INTRODUCED thus far are taken from everyday life and work. In this chapter, the examples we use are on a global and state level and in the context of ethical and moral choices. Ethics and morality amplify the sense of commitment to one's own perspective and "truth" and have considerable consequences for security—at the personal, local, national and global levels.

For many years, the U.S. and Iran have been enemies. They were not always enemies; in fact, they were allies and politically aligned when the Shah was in power. Then, the politics of Iran changed and the U.S. and Iran had a falling out. The language they began using toward each other and when describing each other turned ugly. The stories told of each other portrayed the U.S. as the "Great Satan" and Iran as part of an "Axis of Evil."

The Serpentine Model—introduced in a previous chapter—is useful for depicting the sequence of events that represents the U.S.-Iran relationship story. The Serpentine Model captures the flow of interactions between one or more parties and between those parties and the context within which the events occur. In the following diagram, we depict a high level overview of the historical flow of events that highlights the U.S.- Iran relationship from before the Shah took power to today.

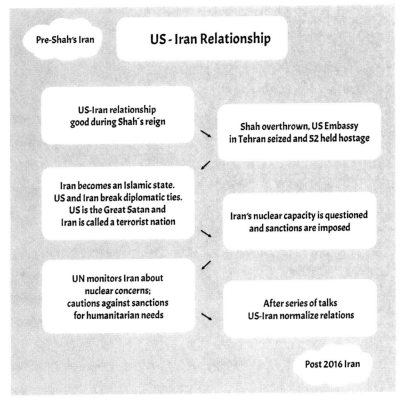

Figure Twelve: Serpentine Model of US-Iran relations

We wanted to present the model in its simplest form. Other CMM models could have been added to it so that, at every turn in the flow of events, there would be further exploration of the phenomenon of the turn. For example, the Daisy Model would capture the influences on a particular event; the LUUUUTT Model would capture the multiple stories in play at the time; a Hierarchy Model could show the levels of context and how they relate to other levels; while another Serpentine Model would show even more detail about a subset of events, or episodes, taking place within the larger sequence.

Now, after many years of vitriol affecting the political climate around the world, the U.S. and Iran have moved past their impasse in an attempt to normalize relations. What does this mean for those directly and indirectly involved? How can these countries be friends one day, enemies the next, and then friends again? What are the stories told that make these shifts?

One of the challenges in high profile and high stakes talks, is that the narratives spun over time make the talks and normalizing relations difficult. In Iran, the U.S. has been portrayed as the Great Satan; everything affiliated with it is evil. In the United States, the narrative about Iran is that of a rogue state and a supporter of terrorism, while the U.S. is actively committed to the Global War on Terror (GWOT). These carefully crafted meta-narratives have been spun so tightly that they have become the dominant narratives and allow little or no room for alternative perspectives. They are deeply entrenched in the minds of all who have been living within them. These entrenched narratives constitute the ethnocentric form of communication because, while there is recognition of difference and judgment on each side, the storytelling is that one's own narrative is the correct one. How can these relations and further talks progress in good faith, with trust that the parties will carry out whatever agreements they reach, when— according to the existing narratives—Iran will be collaborating with the Great Satan and the U.S. will be collaborating with a supporter of state-sanctioned terrorism?

Regardless of whether these portrayals are true, accurate, or valid, these intentional frames are created to make patterns of communication that support certain belief systems and every action highlighted further supports those established beliefs. This is characteristic of what we do when we listen to new information and, in the process of making meaning, try to find a place for it in our current belief systems.

Global affairs are but one scenario with "us" and "them" narratives that we experience in our everyday lives. Consider disparaging comments made about family members because they do not fit into the norms and "shoulds" of the rest of the family. Perhaps there are students in school or families in neighborhoods who seem different because of the way they look, the clothes they wear, or the foods they eat. These "us" and "them" narratives are created and perpetuated in our families, our schools, our communities, and in the media.

If we compare narratives that brand us and them, we can notice some common characteristics. One characteristic is that fear and suspicion is usually embedded in the descriptions of the other, which can be subtly hidden or apparent. The explanations of differences may not be factual, but come to be believed because they are the only explanations given. They are used so often and consistently that we buy into and believe them because they become the norm. This is a pattern across narratives. As humans, we look for ways to understand our world because the unknown can be scary and unpredictable. Too often, we find the closest explanation and latch onto it without looking deeper. This reflects our need for coherence—as discussed earlier—as one of the underlying principles of CMM. Emotions are linked to our communication and we continue to foster emotional reactions that are reflected in the language we use and the way we communicate.

Creating new patterns may take some extra effort at first. Once the patterns are established, they are easier to manifest and take on a life of their own as they build momentum. We no longer even consider doing any fact finding to confirm their validity because we have used them for so long that they are familiar and comfortable. For example, the first time we walk through a field of high grass we need to lift our feet up high. After several walks, the grass becomes matted down and a path is formed making it easier to walk on this path; we exert less effort. Going forward, when we think about reaching point B from point A we will take the established path we created. The same is true for thinking about the image and actions of the U.S. or Iran, depending on which country's framing we use to view the other country.

Similar patterns are being created in recent narratives of people fleeing their war-torn countries. In some stories, they are referred to as migrants, in others as refugees, or still others as immigrants. The terminology that is chosen has legal implications and implicative force that reflect the orientation of who should accept them and provide for them. Some places are building fences and shutting their doors, while others feel a moral responsibility to make provisions. These responses are forms of "speech acts." We can look at the values and beliefs influencing which speech acts are made and, in turn, what they make in the process. Fear, in the form of xenophobia, abounds in these crafted narratives of "what they will do to our homes if we let them in." The human needs of safety and security are being threatened by difference and, in many cases, the narratives reflect this fear of other.

In the next diagram we show how the LUUUUTT Model—the storytelling model—can be used to explore the multiple stories informing current conversations and references about the U.S.—Iran relationship. This is particularly useful as a way to map our current assumptions, identify gaps in our knowledge, and raise questions of what we need to query to gain deeper understanding. It allows us to differentiate between what we know, what we think we know, and what we need to know.

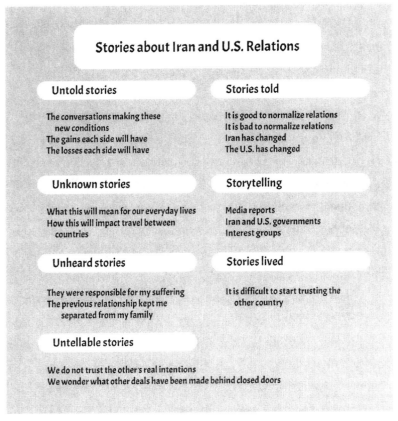

Figure Thirteen: The LUUUUTT Model about Iran and U.S. relations

The stories we tell frame the dynamics and perpetuate the logical forces that create the scenes from which certain actions follow. For example, if there is a terrorist act in the Middle East, Western media will likely mention Iran as a possible contributor, regardless of whether it has been confirmed. This is classified as prefigurative force because a particular action sparks a following action. This leads to a reinforced narrative that Iran supports terrorism and leads to comments like "See, there they go again." This comment perpetuates and validates the narrative of Iran as a terrorist state. The U.S. may generate more of this type of rhetoric to increase support for continued sanctions or other actions against Iran; this would be considered practical force as a response to Iran's support of terrorism. The pattern that has been established reinforces the narrative, which is then perceived to be true.

Our perceptions are our reality, so it is small "t" truth for us. If the UN takes certain actions or places certain constraints, the U.S. can decide whether to support the actions. This is influenced by contextual force: whether the U.S. considers itself a member of the international community (support the UN) or the global police force (take actions independently). The context is further complicated by the process of weighing multiple perspectives on choices and implications in both the U.S. and Iran.

After so many years of deeply embedded narrative patterns of the U.S. being the great Satan, or Iran being the supporter of terrorism, suddenly shifting this narrative will not be easy for most of the population to initially support. This new framing of the other is so contrary to what has been previously believed and propagated and the former patterns have been so deeply ingrained in the psyche and mindset, that to declare that the two countries will now be working together and trusting the other to abide by this new agreement is a complete 180° turn. If we want to change the existing patterns and the scenarios, we need to create episodes that generate implicative forces.

The implicative forces we create become the next set of prefigurative forces. In this example, reframing Iran from terrorist to ally or the U.S. from Satan to ally, shifts perspectives of the Iran-U.S. relationship and the subsequent new narratives being created. Shifting perspectives, particularly when there are very strong contrary forces, can be very challenging and is what has disrupted previous attempts at normalizing relations.

These polarized narratives are ethnocentric forms of communication. These types of stories reflect what is happening now and will continue into the predictable future in many areas of our lives. As long as we perpetuate these polarizing narratives, we continue our pattern of ethnocentric communication and perpetuate untrusting relational processes. We will not be able to embrace a new relational dynamic, we will not trust the other side, and any agreements we come to or actions we intend to take will either fail or require terrific scrutiny at every step of the way.

CMM provides the tools and conceptual frameworks to guide us in shifting the form of communication we use, from ethnocentric to modernistic and, ideally, cosmopolitan. Communication does not happen in a vacuum; it is an active interaction between two or more parties who are engaging in creating shared meaning. The influences on shaping the communication come from those involved, the stories and past interactions, the context within which we are communicating, and many other influences. This creates the system within which meaning is being made. It is a system because the interplay amongst these various sources of influence continue to alter and shape the meaning being made while integrating feedback from previous interactions. This continuous cycle may shift when new information is introduced into the existing system. Meaning can be transformed if the new influences are disruptive enough to cause the otherwise deeply embedded established narrative pattern to shift.

The following Hierarchy Model depicts the shifting levels of context that reflect U.S. perspectives on Iran. The highest level of the hierarchy in the diagrams is the U.S.'s priority of the need for security. This is a strong mindset that cannot be challenged, so it influences everything that is embedded within it. As the highest level of context, it has the most strength and is therefore the biggest predictor of behavior. The subtle shifts happen in the lower levels of context in which the U.S. view of Iran moves from a black and white classification of Iran supporting terror, to Iran not always being a direct threat. This subtle, but impactful, shift leaves room for shades of grey in regards to whether Iranian actions are directly linked to acts of terrorism.

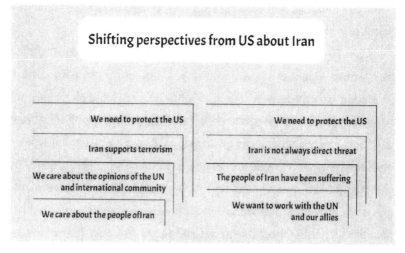

Shifting perspectives from US about Iran

We need to protect the US	We need to protect the US
Iran supports terrorism	Iran is not always direct threat
We care about the opinions of the UN and international community	The people of Iran have been suffering
We care about the people of Iran	We want to work with the UN and our allies

Figure Fourteen: Shifting perspectives between Iran and the U.S

One of the goals when creating shared meaning is to coordinate with others to feel connection and receive social recognition. Coordination, as one of the principles of CMM, is based on the belief that we create the social worlds within which we live by building relationships with others. The nature of these relationships influences the quality of the social worlds we create. Humans are wired to connect with others and we are intrinsically rewarded when we are collaborative.[22] Being in coordination and creating shared meaning is an act of collaboration. When we are not in

Meaning can be transformed if the new influences are disruptive enough to cause the otherwise deeply embedded established narrative pattern to shift.

coordination with others, we have dissonance between us that creates the type of social world within which we do not want to live. We have agency over the types of social worlds we want to create—more than we think we do.

In referencing the Iran—U.S. nuclear talks, the interpretation of what is transpiring and the subsequent actions is shaped by the way we frame "the other." When we coordinate meaning making, we can be in sync with each other and derive similar enough understandings to cooperate. This sometimes means that we need to transcend an ethnocentric form of communication that keeps us separate and fearful to foster relational processes that enable us to create the space in which to coordinate shared meaning making. As noted earlier, expanding how we name the episode we are engaged in, and co-creating and highlighting what we are making, can potentially shift the form of communication we use. Naming the episode is a way of looking at what and how the actions and meanings are emerging. Looking at the episode makes the patterns of communication we are making more explicit. In so doing, we may see new aspects of the episode and the communication. This new information gives us an opportunity to change the dynamics with new actions that create practical forces. In ethnocentric communication (as well as in monocultural and modernistic forms), many assumptions remain unnamed and implicit.

There is no awareness of the other in monocultural communication, so there is no felt need to name something because it is not even recognized as existing. Instead, there is an assumption that only one narrative exists. In cosmopolitan communication, assumptions also exist but they are noticed and there is more intention to surface and address them. In ethnocentric communication, the narrative of self and other is rigid and polarized. This elicits certain types of behaviors that create patterns of communication that do not foster productive coordination. The prefigurative forces of these types of communication do not lead toward useful and nuanced coordination and shared meaning making, but rather perpetuate polarization. By naming the actions that become episodes, we surface the assumptions and make the implicit, explicit. Once made explicit, the assumptions can be changed and thus create yet another, perhaps more generative, turn in the relationship.

...expanding how we name the episode we are engaged in, and co-creating and highlighting what we are making, can potentially shift the form of communication we use.

Once these episodes are named and the frames made explicit, we have an opportunity to unpack them. Episodes are complex and there are many elements that create them. These elements become so intertwined and integrated with one another it is difficult to see where one element begins and another ends. We use the term "unpack" to suggest that when we open the episode, as in opening a suitcase or backpack, we begin to take out the items that were stuffed inside. The act of unpacking separates the items, or in this case elements, so that we may view each of them in isolation and then in combination with one another.

We can have conversations about what these episodes make and how that serves the people making them. We act in ways that satisfy our needs whether we are conscious of it, even if our actions may be destructive. On some occasions, what is being made fosters fear of the other. When under external pressure to modify our behaviors—so that we do not create and perpetuate fear—we need to first recognize what we are doing (or not doing) that is perceived as fear inducing. We and the other can then explore how to shift our framing and behaviors to address the fear and reduce the threat the other perceives.

Naming perceptions and assumptions and how they link to behaviors is necessary and worthwhile if there is to be a shift from an ethnocentric form of communication. We need to develop a level of self-awareness that supports us wanting to experience this exploration and a shared commitment and motivation with others to engage in reflective conversations to make these shifts. The communication perspective and the heuristics or tools of CMM

> *Naming perceptions and assumptions and how they link to behaviors is necessary and worthwhile if there is to be a shift from an ethnocentric form of communication.*

support our capacity to both look at and be in the conversation at the same time.

In this chapter, we highlighted the following:

➤ We create patterns of communication to support and reinforce our belief systems.

➤ Multiple CMM models can be used together to explore different aspects of the patterns of communication that we make in each interaction or event.

➢ We need to change the "us" and "them" narratives created to reinforce differences if we want to transcend ethnocentric communication patterns.

➢ Implicative logical forces can change the trajectory of existing narratives.

➢ Meaning is made in the interactions within a system.

➢ We create our social worlds in relationship when we coordinate with others.

CHAPTER 5: ENGAGING
It Isn't All Personal—Taking a System View
(NOREN)

IN OUR COACHING RELATIONSHIPS, clients often bring up the issue of taking things personally. In this chapter, we expand on how the communication perspective provides a walking stick to guide reflection in action to support a systems view and to see oneself in the context of systems dynamics. Our use of the term "systems" refers to the inter-relatedness of people and relationships with boundaries and connections. Each subsystem provides a context from which interactions and meaning making are derived. So, if a client is interpreting situations from a personal perspective, that is the aspect of the system on which they are focusing. The other individual(s) in the interaction may not be referring to that person's "personhood," but rather their role and rank within an organizational context. For them it is not personal, rather work related. In the same situation, with the same persons interacting, different meanings are drawn depending on each person's perspective.

The many levels of context within and across systems are consequential to how we make sense of a moment, an episode, and relationships, in general. For example, when we are with our family, contexts may include birth order, age, gender, and other aspects of relational connection. The contexts of family are embedded in our many communities, (i.e., geographic neighborhood, religious community, schools, workplaces, etc.) which in turn are embedded in larger social systems.

Many conversations, as though with forces of their own, take turns we do not expect. We do not have complete control over the ebb and flow of turn-taking and the direction of the conversation, despite what we think or hope. We often do not anticipate these forces, but they become apparent to us when we bump into them, seemingly by chance, because they put up unexpected barriers. For example, we might take for granted that we are just beginning a conversation when something from the past, that we thought was long buried, surfaces. The Serpentine Model helps us look at this turn where something unexpected appears. In the flow of our conversations, we are most inclined to expect that those who are present and directly engaged will be the ones who are influencing and making meaning. However, others who are not physically present or directly engaged also influence the meaning making that emerges in the back and forth of the conversation. This is because our life experiences, the cultural and contextual influences of where we are and where we have been, all play a role in shaping how we communicate with others and the meaning we make from those interactions. In other words, we—and others—are embedded in multiple systems at any given time and these systems influence how we make meaning together. Contexts inform not only what is overtly done, but also how one understands what the other has done, is doing and is anticipated to do.

Our experiences create what we can refer to as *meaning frames*, which are the frameworks or lenses we use to interpret and make meaning from the world around us; specifically, the systems to which we are referring. In today's world, which is referred to by some as being postmodern, there is no longer an overarching meta-narrative, or shared narrative by which we all live. Our interactions have increased in frequency and speed. Shorter turnaround times and advances in technology have diminished impediments due to geographical distance. Therefore, we have more and more occasions to interface with others who may have different meaning making frames or lenses and more opportunities for our different narratives to collide. In the next section, we explore how communication takes place in these different levels or systems simultaneously, how they interact with one another, and how we can better create shared meaning.

Examples of multiple system levels include intrapersonal, interpersonal, intragroup, intergroup, team, organizational, societal, global, etc. These levels of subsystems co-exist and move so that any particular subsystem may move to the forefront at any given moment, while the others recede into the background. Because they are dynamic, there is a continuous flow of movement across levels of subsystems.

Various forces influence how these systems and subsystems move between foreground and background. Some we cause by paying attention to certain aspects of our lives and environments, while others may be stimulated by external factors, such as new policies and practices in the workplace, legal status, or contracts. Consider the instance of a woman who was asked to meet a friend for lunch. Initially, her response was based on whether she could take the time off work and find a mutually convenient place to meet. In this case, context and logistics were primary considerations. When her friend added that she was dealing with a crisis and needed her counsel, the story of self (as responsive friend) and relationship became primary. Another example is a client who is a German citizen working in London. Recently, he was considering a promotion at the company he has worked with for over 10 years. Initially, he was negotiating the contract foregrounding his experience, his performance and his status on the team. In a matter of days, the dynamics of the contexts shifted as a consequence of the UK's decision to leave the European Union and the contractual ramifications of that decision.

We are constantly engaged in a process of creating coherence, of trying to align what is happening with how we make sense of things. Every day, there seems to be yet another tragic story in the news, the meaning of which shifts as the storytelling unfolds and more context is added. We have a need to understand the stories we hear. Sometimes, we do not have the patience to wait and listen to how the story may unfold before we generate a list of questions to probe further. The desire for coherence ignites a desire to know and our impatience can be a result of our inability to manage the ambiguity of not knowing. Eventually, the next piece of context is reported and, while that may satisfy some of our curiosity, there may be other information we still want to know. In a matter of time, as more and more information is revealed, we realize the complexity of the story. The more we know, the more we realize what we don't know and so it continues.

One such story unfolded in the U.S. in Orlando, Florida on June 11, 2016. This event was considered to be the worst mass shooting in U.S. history, leaving 49 people dead and 53 wounded. The unfolding information from the news was not as coherent as it might seem in retrospect. The breaking news at 11pm EST June 11th was of a shooting in a bar. For some, the highest context for understanding this event was *gun control*: those who support gun control may have thought—here we go again—this is the consequence of the widespread availability of guns. Then, the story unfolded:

- The next morning, we learned that the location of the shooting was a gay bar. The defining context shifts to violence against the LGBTQ population. The news also reported that bar was hosting its weekly "Upscale Latin Saturdays" party, raising the question as to whether members of the Latin gay community were specifically targeted.

- Then the news reported that the shooter was Omar Mateen, a Muslim, and that he called emergency services to pledge his allegiance to the leader of the Islamic State of Iraq and the Levant (ISIL), Abu Bakr al-Baghadi. The defining context shifts to issues of immigration that have been in the news and whether the solution is to close off our borders despite the report that Mateen was born in New York, USA.

- The next story told was about a man (Mateen) who had lost a series of security-related and law enforcement jobs due to threats of bringing a gun. His first wife left him after a matter of months because, she reported, "he was mentally unstable and mentally ill" and "obviously disturbed deeply, and traumatized and was often physically abusive." The context now shifts to one of mental illness.

- Then the stories about his relationships with gay men, trolling gay websites, and questioning his sexual orientation became the focus.

In each turn, the logical force is a desire for certainty and a clear explanation that will provide us with coherence. If only we had a clear explanation, we can anticipate the next tragedy; if only we knew who to blame, we would be able to assure ourselves that we can protect ourselves from it happening again.

The context of the 2016 presidential election elevated the logical force of the storytelling. Each turn, each explanation, from violence and gun control, to homophobia, to racism, to islamophobia and terrorism, to mental illness and people who are mentally ill having access to firearms, all trigger election rhetoric. At each step of the way, we draw conclusions in our attempts at sense making. We may feel a sense of dissonance if the information we are trying to comprehend does not fit or we cannot make it fit with our existing frames of reference, information, and understanding. Unfortunately, because we do not like the feeling of dissonance, we grasp the first explanation that makes sense to us and that brings us a semblance of coherence, even if the information is not accurate. While dissonance may feel uncomfortable, it is part of the process of learning and growing.

There are differing degrees and durations of discomfort we are willing to manage and many ways in which we engage dissonance. One, is to sort the incoming information to align it with our current way of knowing. In the case of the Orlando shooting, if we believe shootings are random and shooters are terrorists and terrorists are Muslim and Muslims are foreign born, then we attend to information that identifies the shooter as a Muslim terrorist. When new information about the shooter reveals that he grew up in a town on Long Island, New York and that his first wife thought he was mentally ill, the storytelling becomes more complex.

An example of this is how we may minimize painful events or how we remember conversations. We may disregard and reject parts of the information completely because it is too radically different from what we "know" and we would need to change our existing meaning frames to be able to accept it. Changing existing meaning frames is a significant undertaking.

At the interpersonal level of context, we aspire to create shared meaning and coordinate our understanding of the world and each other. At a minimum, we are looking to be safe and survive. On a more sophisticated level, we are looking to grow and thrive and thus reach more of our potential. We do this through communication in relationship; we seek the other as an aid to our growth and this may lead to transformation. Daloz,[23] an adult educator, identifies *engaging with the other* as one of four conditions for transformation. When we transform our perspectives by taking in information from a broader span of sources, we grow. On the other hand, our perspective may impede our development and the dynamic may even reach the extremes of becoming dependent on or, feeling threatened by, the other. All of this occurs in communication between and among us within a particular context, in relationship to others.

While meaning creation happens *between* us, we also need to keep in mind that meaning making is simultaneously happening *within* us. As I interact with you, take in information from what you say and the context in which you say it, then make meaning from it based on my understanding of what I "know" to be true, I am deciding how this fits with my existing meaning frames. If your communication resonates with me, we are engaging in shared meaning making. However, if I am experiencing dissonance I must determine how to respond. We often do not realize that our responses are a choice; often, we react with what feels like instinct or an automatic response. We can accept what you are saying and live with the dissonance, we can reject what you are saying because it does not fit with our meaning frames, or we can challenge you on your ideas and, perhaps, be in conflict.

The group and intergroup levels have similar dynamics that happen within and between groups. Shared stories of the way the world is and how it should be are common to the group and bind it together as a cohesive unit. The narratives of different groups can complement each other, coexist, or compete. In the case of competitive or rival group dynamics, the dissonance may threaten the narrative that binds the group causing feelings of external threat, which may cause the group to become even more cohesive and wedded to their shared narrative.

Interactions with other groups also reflectively shape the narratives we form. Groups that share in the same struggle continue to weave shared events into their narratives, thus forging stronger bonds and coherence amongst the group members and fostering feelings of home and community. Inadvertently, this may also work to strengthen in-group/out-group dynamics, "us and them," because those not sharing in the memorable events that form strong relationship bonds are outside of the particular group that shared the events. An example of this is when group members develop a shortcut to remembering an event and have the same events in common as reference points of shared experiences—an "inside joke."

Other levels of systems are greater in size and scope than those previously mentioned; organizations, nation states, regions of the world, and continents, for example. They, of course, are made of smaller systems and are therefore, by this very nature, more complex.

Each of these levels is a mini-system and has contextual forces that define how meaning is made and processed. The context of our group contains certain norms and values of the way we function as a group, who belongs, what we are supposed to do, etc. When we interact with other groups, they may have some overlapping norms and values or none at all. We need to find ways to understand the contextual forces at work in both groups so we can collaborate in shared meaning making or we may end up in conflict.

The Hierarchy Model is useful for identifying the different levels of systems within which we are operating and to further identify the contextual forces within and between these systems. Using the Hierarchy Model also allows us to see how one system is embedded in another and how the foregrounded system facilitates dynamic shifts between the different levels of the hierarchy.

In the figure below we show that, in this particular system of four mini-systems or levels, family is the foreground to work, school, and community. The contextual forces of being a member of this particular family are stronger than the contextual forces of the other three categories.

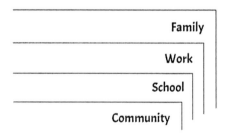

Figure Fifteen: Hierarchy Model with family as the foreground

If there were to be a change in circumstances and the community level required strong participation to help pass a referendum, community would shift in importance and rise to the top of the Hierarchy. The contextual forces surrounding the community system would then have a stronger influence.

77

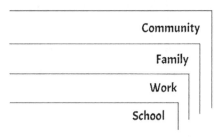

Figure Sixteen: Hierarchy Model with community as the foreground

In another shift of priorities, perhaps an assignment is due at school; school as a context shifts to figure prominently. In this case the contextual forces of being a student in school are stronger than family, work, or community.

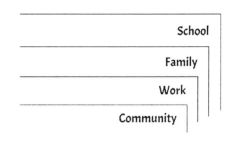

Figure Seventeen: Hierarchy Model with school being in the foreground

Our lives are fluid and the different sets of systems shift many times within any given day based on what we are doing, whom we are with, and where we are. Each of these levels provides many different forces that influence how meaning is made.

In this chapter, we highlighted the following:

➢ Systems are the interrelatedness of people and relationships with boundaries and connections.

➢ We create meaning frames to make meaning of the world around us.

➢ Subsystems are embedded within broader systems.

➢ Systems are dynamic and different aspects of the system become foregrounded when we pay more attention to them.

➢ Stories, context, and meaning making shift as we learn more information.

➢ Meaning making happens between and within us simultaneously.

CHAPTER 6: NOTICING (AGAIN)
From Reflex to Intention
Creating Possibilities (NOREN)

IN THE PREVIOUS CHAPTERS, we focused on how meaning is continuously emerging in social, relational processes by highlighting different aspects of the meaning making process: noticing (N), observing (O), reflecting (R), and engaging (E).

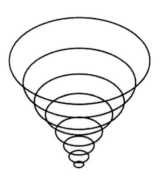

Figure Eighteen: *NOREN*

These processes are not linear; rather they are like a spiral coming back to a particular episode with new perspectives. In this chapter, we build on the reflective spiral coming back to noticing with new perspectives. Sometimes these new perspectives come from another person.

We have a client who hates to drive in traffic. His demeanor transforms when there is a driver in his midst who is not following his rules, which is why the following story was particularly amusing.

"I was driving on the local four-lane when I found this driver in front particularly annoying. I should know better, but I was about to make a hand gesture—a gesture to correspond to the look of frustration on my face—when my spouse quickly noted that the driver was a neighbor. At once, I changed the gesture from one that would have been quite rude, to a wave."

This story has resonance with many people across many cultures. It is a story of everyday life and its annoyances. It is a story of how often we find ourselves enmeshed in overlapping, unraveling, unfinished webs of perceived "oughtness"—because he did this, we must do that. It is also a story about how we can shift an episode of insult to greeting in a matter of seconds—just by noticing. Noticing involves looking at our own behaviors and what we are making; what we are creating moment by moment. Noticing expands the choices we make and the possibilities we create. Noticing often requires the perspective of another for us to expand our own meaning making process.

Yet, all too often, we make assumptions and draw conclusions based on incomplete and impartial information. We engage in habits of forms of communication that are deeply rooted in stories of self-protection; taking for granted that we know more than them and that they are wrong and we are right. Referring back to some of the previous scenarios, Reema and her co-workers made assumptions about each other that morning in the staff room. There was a disorienting event: a bombing attack in Paris. People were afraid and relationships shifted. In the stories of Halima and Karen and of Jeremy and Joanna, assumptions were also made about each other—each with different provocations. In a sense, we are always making assumptions with incomplete information.

Our views are incomplete; we depend on each other to add layers, textures, and nuances to our storytelling. The layers continuously add to the richness and the depth with stories that may not have been told, heard, known, or even allowed. When we revisit the episode of Halima and Karen, we learn that Karen addressed her discomfort in not telling Halima the whole story. In a follow-up conversation with Halima, she shared the untold story of how she arranged an alternative ride to the airport and her regret at not addressing it more fully when they were together. Her logic was based in her own cultural rules: there is dissonance if you want to have a fully authentic relationship when you have not been fully honest. In sharing this with Halima, she learned that her concerns were her own. Halima had sensed there was more to the story—and it did not matter to her. What mattered was that they had each gone out of their way to spend time together. What mattered to her was that Karen came to her town to learn about her work and see it firsthand. What mattered to her was the common view of the future to which they were committed. An episode that Karen may have initiated to "clear the air" turned into another level of learning about someone else's cultural lens and, in so doing, learning about her own assumptions.

The story our colleague told about the car ride with Ed was also incomplete. When we asked permission to use this episode in this book, our colleague reviewed the version of the story told here with Ed. Ironically, each had a somewhat different version; each credited the other with suggesting they arrange for a car service. Each had their own story of what led up to the conversation, the conversation they anticipated, and their respective rules of engagement. This is probably not surprising. Perhaps, more often than not, we find that the memory we have of an event or an encounter is different from those with whom we shared the experience. This serves as a reminder that the meaning we create together is an ongoing process. As we seek to create coordination and coherence with others, we need to continuously notice the assumptions we are making, the narratives we craft, and how our frames and narratives influence the actions we choose.

One of the challenges we face in making explicit all of the assumptions we hold and the cultural influences that create them, is that there are different rules to what should and should not be explicit. Cultures have different boundaries for what is public and what is private and there are logical forces guiding us to know what these are within our own cultural perspectives. Therefore, it is not clear to what level we should make our thoughts, feelings, and beliefs known. In the example of Karen and Halima, they were able to share in the overarching goal of making the world a better place and that goal was elevated in the shared hierarchy they were creating together. Prior to that telephone call, each was operating according to her hierarchies and elevating what was important to her. They had coherence within themselves about their stories of what happened and their relationship. They did not have coordination until aligning their priorities during the telephone call.

CMM as social construction

At its roots, CMM is based in social constructionism. Gergen[24] describes social constructionism as an amalgam of three dialogues that originated in separate lines of study. One is that our values create our descriptions of reality. Thus, we must account for what constitutes value assumptions. The second dialogue is that making sense is a matter of adhering to the rules of language. The third contributing dialogue, and the most impactful according to Gergen, is that scientific knowledge can be thought of as a byproduct of social process. One common example is the construction of time that now dominates our life. The construction of time, in turn, creates the situation of being early, late, or on time. These differ across cultures. Values are culture specific as are the rules of language usage and the meanings we assign to time.

The patterns of communication in which we are engaged are habits that are repeated over time and are often not clearly or fully noticeable or articulated. Taking the observer, or third-person, perspective helps make the patterns more explicit. From this stance, we can assess whether the communication patterns we are making in our relational processes are helpful, neutral or harmful.

Throughout the book, we have looked at how the tools and frameworks of CMM help us look at the patterns we are creating in the relational aspects of the meaning making process. Where these patterns are helpful, we want to notice what they create in order to replicate them. If they are harmful, we want to identify the ways in which we can transform them into more constructive patterns. For example, The Serpentine Model helps us address disruptive communication patterns by capturing the flow of a conversation, identifying the turns taken by the participants, and introducing a turn that creates a more virtuous—rather than vicious—cycle. We can then identify the critical moments when the serpentine thread of our conversation took different turns. We can use the Daisy and the Hierarchy Models to look at what each person was prioritizing as a way to clarify the assumptions from which they were acting.

The form of noticing we are suggesting requires some effort in looking at the patterns we create. Davidson[25] talks about the six dimensions of emotional style: self-awareness, social intuition, context, resilience, outlook, and attention, which we will explore here. The naming and framing of these styles resonates with what we commonly refer to as emotional and social intelligence. Naming the styles enables us to look at their dimensions and consider how they support our process of noticing and making choices. *Self-awareness* is noticing oneself. In what ways am I noticing my internal and external responses? How intentional and mindful are my responses regarding what I want to create with another?

A colleague was taking her teenage son to university for the first time. Her primary focus was on being a supportive parent to her son as he was making this important transition. She was focused on helping him unpack, engaging his roommate in conversation, etc. As she shared the story, she recalled the moment she moved her perspective from *being* in the moment to *looking at* the moment. In so doing, she noticed that she was lingering and that her son was being too polite to let her know it was time for her to leave. As she noticed this, she shifted the most important context from being with him in this transition to supporting his move toward independence.

Social intuition is about noticing and sensing the other. In the case of our colleague, noticing that her son was ready to move into the next episode—meeting new people and getting settled—was a critical turn. *Context* is noticing the rules of the particular social context and adapting your response accordingly while *attending* is about how you focus. In this case, the social rules have an implicative force of parents saying goodbye and getting in the car!

Resilience speaks to how quickly we recover from setbacks or adversity. First, how well do we notice our response to things not going the way we had hoped or planned? To what extent do we attribute similar significance to a friend changing a dinner engagement and learning about a significant medical diagnosis that will entail an involved intervention? How do we look at our resilience in a manner that leads to creating more of it? We have all had situations where the news was unexpected or potentially unpleasant. Yet, when something is named and framed, there are physical, emotional, spiritual, and other avenues to explore. *Outlook* shows up as our tendency to focus on the strengths or positive aspects of a situation or to instead focus on the limitations and challenges. Noticing our outlook opens alternatives for storytelling.

On August 19, 2016, Esther walked out of her house and was startled by the disturbing sight of a swastika on her trashcan. She looked around and noticed that her neighbor's homes were untouched.[26] After calling the police, she called her neighbors. Initially she described her response as simultaneously "furious, scared, and sad". And then, one of her neighbors and good friends reminded Esther about what she stood for: "Don't give this person, who made you feel angry and unsafe, the power ... Nothing conquers hate more than love. Do something to turn it around," he said.

Taking a cue from an initiative called Paintback, where German artists have transformed neo-Nazi images, including some 50 swastikas into "fanciful" figures, he encouraged Esther to do the same. Another friend suggested painting a smiley face over the swastika.

An artist by profession, Esther took her paints outside and transformed the swastika into a beautiful orange pinwheel flower. She then posted photos on Facebook and distributed flyers to neighbors explaining the situation. She made an open invitation and instructions on how to participate, thus extending the context from a personal episode to a community one, and from an insult to generative message.

"I am asking you, in this neighborhood and beyond ... to paint something positive on your trash cans. We can, in our little way, turn this symbol of hate into something beautiful ... anything your imagination can come up with.

"The only criteria is to start with this negative symbol, the swastika, and make it positive," she wrote.

Literally, within minutes, people began texting, emailing and posting on her on Facebook. Images of trash cans covered top to bottom with peace symbols, "No Place for Hate" slogans, butterflies, flower gardens, expressions of love, and more poured in from near and far, including the United Kingdom, Canada and Germany. Her friend and their 12-year-old son, turned swastikas into Ferris wheels, a portrait of their Boxer and a rendition of the Philadelphia LOVE sculpture.

Esther said the overwhelming response has reinforced her sense of an inclusive community where "Everyone has my back ... It felt like everyone couldn't believe this outrageous thing happened. Everyone turned it around and made it positive." Painting the swastika was a "stupid act," she said. "But I really want to believe that people in my community aren't like that."

In a critical moment, Esther made a choice. She could have focused on insult and alienation, but instead made a turn that created community and affirmations. She could have focused on trying to find out the perpetrator's identity, but instead, in her own words said, "I'd rather give the power to the people who are rising up and making it positive."

As we notice, observe, reflect, and engage, the language and framing of how we construct our social worlds is continuously unfolding. The communication perspective that CMM embraces sees other ways of framing human interaction, as additional enhancements to our understanding. The act of noticing again allows us to directly influence how our minds work. The use of CMM and taking a communication perspective provides opportunities for us to come from a place of deeper knowledge and understanding of multiple perspectives. This in turn gets reinforced when we do notice again and the cycle continues as we make new patterns of com-

> *The communication perspective that CMM embraces sees other ways of framing human interaction, as additional enhancements to our understanding.*

munication. In other words, there is a direct connection between the patterns we are observing and how we construct our social worlds in the space between us in relationship.

In this chapter, we highlighted the following:

➢ We notice, observe, reflect, engage, and notice (NOREN) in a reflective spiral.

➢ Reflection invites the exploration of what we hope, fear, anticipate, expect, desire, and so on.

➢ Critical moments are crossroads where the force of our choices are particularly consequential.

➢ Our individual views are incomplete and they become more enriched when we co-create stories with others.

➢ CMM tools and frameworks enable us to look at the communication patterns we are creating.

CHAPTER 7: SUMMARY AND REFLECTIONS

When some things are called beautiful, other things become ugly.

When some things are called good, other things become bad.

Being and nonbeing create each other.

Difficult and easy support each other.

Long and short define each other.

High and low depend upon each other.

Before and after follow each other.

~ Tao Te Ching

IN THE JOURNEY OF WRITING this book, there have been many twists and turns—some challenging and others more enriching. The seeds of this book were planted in conversation with Barnett Pearce. The intention of this book was to be an accessible path to the theory and practice of CMM. In the process, Barnett was diagnosed with an aggressive form of cancer. As he engaged with his mortality and his legacy, his writing about the evolution of CMM expanded in unanticipated ways both individually and with Kim Pearce.[27] As we wrote this book, our clear focus was to engage you, the reader, with CMM as an everyday practice and its applications for daily interactions at work and home as well as for research and reflection.

Stories are the means by which we create shared meaning and, we see over and over again, examples of how our stories are always unfolding—shifting—turning. Each time we began to write a story as a channel for describing a model, the story was altered in some way by the next turn. We are humbled by the anticipation of the stories that will unfold tomorrow and the next day that will recontextualize this book.

CMM is in our bones. We, no doubt, were living the model we were writing and writing the model we were living. We do hope that this book enhances the initiatives of our colleagues and friends who walk with us in sharing the value of CMM and the communication perspective in making better social worlds. We hope that the tools and frameworks provide the walking stick, the railings, that help to steady us in a world where the speed of change all too often has us breathless.

We also want to offer that this is one set of suggestions of how to understand CMM and take a communication perspective. In every example we explored, there were multiple other ways of explaining and interpreting waiting in the wings. In every example we explored, there were multiple other ways of explaining and interpreting CMM and the communication perspective waiting in the wings. This was our turn in the unfolding of this conversation. Now it is your turn.

GLOSSARY

Circular questioning.

Questions that focus on the relationships rather than facts. The questions probe differences between and among people and events

Daisy Model

The Daisy Model highlights the various conversations and influences that are related to a person, episode or event. The model, named for the shape, helps to look at what conversations are considered or valued and what else might be helpful to consider to expand meaning.

Episodes

Episodes are an artificial boundary that mark the beginning, middle and end of a stream of events. Defining episodes is one way of supporting the process of looking at our interactions and what we are making together.

Hierarchy Model

The Hierarchy Model depicts the many contexts that shape meaning. The model guides one's attention to many contexts that are influencing the meaning of the episode, how the contexts are nested, and our taken for granted assumptions.

Logical Force

Logal Force is the sense of "oughtness" that propels what we do, particularly in joint action with others. There are different kinds of logical forces:

- *Prefigurative force*: a response based on what has just happened;

- *Contextual force*: a response based on the situation in which we are;

- *Practical force*: a response based on what we hope the other person will do; and

- *Implicative*: the effects our actions are intended to have on the contexts in which they occur.

LUUUUTT Model

The LUUUUTT Model, an acronym for stories Lived, stories Untold, stories Unheard, stories Unknown, Unallowable stories, stories Told, and storyTelling, turns our attention to how speech acts are partial, unfolding and interrelated. The stories we tell ourselves about who we are, what we are doing, and the interrelationships we have with others are only a part of the actual social event. This model helps prompt us to probe for what else we might explore, and consequently, hear, learn, invite, give permission to, and so on. The model also calls our attention to the tone and manner of storytelling.

Serpentine Model

The Serpentine Model highlights the flow of events, interactions, and turns of what is said and done between and among people in the multiple contexts of our social interactions. Each turn presents an opportunity, a choice to take any number of directions.

Unwanted Repetitive Pattern

Unwanted Repetitive Patterns (URPs) occur when contextual and prefigurative forces are high and practical and implicative forces are low. URP's happen when people must act in a particular way because of what other people did or are doing.

ENDNOTES

Introduction

1 Pearce, W. B. (2004). The coordinated management of meaning. In W. B. Gudykunst (Ed.), Theorizing about intercultural communication (pp. 35–54). Thousand Oaks, CA: Sage. This is one of the first chapters introducing the Coordinated Management of Meaning.

2 Sigman, S. (1995). The consequentiality of communication, Lawrence Erlbaum Associates, NY: Routledge Press. In this book, Sigman expanded the idea that communication conveys meanings derived from cultural, psychological/cognitive and sociological structures, to the motion that meaning emerges from the communication process itself. Meaning is therefore related to what transpires during the actual moments of engagement.

3 Gergen, K. J. (2009). Relational being: Beyond self and community. New York: Oxford University Press. p. 55.

4 Pearce, W. B. (2007). Making social worlds: A communication perspective. Malden, MA: Blackwell.

Chapter 1

5 McNamee, S., & Gergen, K. (1999). Relational responsibility: Resources for sustainable dialogue. Thousand Oaks, CA: Sage.

6 Pearce, W. B. (2007). Making social worlds: A communication perspective. Malden, MA: Blackwell.

7 Pearce, K., (2012). Compassionate communicating because moments matter: Poetry, prose, and practices .Lulu Enterprises. (pp. 67-76). Kim Pearce describes the essentials of CMM theory with 4 claims:

1. Our communication creates our social worlds. Social worlds are made of interconnections amongst the selves, relationships, organizations, communities, and cultures that we create in and with communication

2. The stories we tell differ from the stories we live. Stories lived are through series of coordinated actions we make with others, and stories told are our attempts at sense-making. CMM is about the coordinated management of meaning to encompass both these types of stories.

3. We get what we make. We are always making things together. This is an enabling statement as it offers up the opportunity to make the next moment better.

4. Get the pattern right and you create better outcomes. Mindfulness in a CMM context means less about the content of what you are saying, but more on what you and others are doing together. This calls on us to be mindful of the relationship and the conversational flow to see what is emerging and what else is possible.

8 Griffin, E. (2014). Coordinated management of meaning (CMM) of W. Barnett Pearce & Vernon Cronen. In E. Griffin (Ed.), A first look at communication (8th ed. ed., pp. 66-81). New York: McGraw-Hill. p. 67.

9 Pearce, K., (2012). Compassionate communicating because moments matter: Poetry, prose, and practices.

Chapter 2

10 Pearce, W. B. (1989). Communication and the human condition. Carbondale: University of Illinois Press. p. 93.

11 Buber, M. (1947). Between man and man (R. G. Smith, Trans.). New York: Routledge.

12 Kegan, R. (1982). The evolving self: Problem and process in human development. Cambridge, Mass.: Harvard University Press.

13 Kegan, R. (1982). The evolving self: Problem and process in human development. Cambridge, Mass.: Harvard University Press, p. 107.

14 Kegan, R. (1994). In over our heads: The mental demands of modern life. Cambridge, Mass.: Harvard University Press.

15 Kegan, R. (1982). The evolving self: Problem and process in human development. Cambridge, Mass.: Harvard University Press; Kegan, R. (1994). In over our heads: The mental demands of modern life. Cambridge, Mass.: Harvard University Press; Kegan, R. (2000). What forms transforms? In J. A. Mezirow (Ed.), Learning as transformation: Critical perspectives on a theory in progress (pp. 35–70). San Francisco: Jossey-Bass.

16 In a play on the title of Kegan's first book: The Evolving Mind, Kegan's own work in adult development continues to evolve reflected in the changes in terminology: Kegan referred to as stages of development in 1982, orders of consciousness in 1994, and forms of mind in 2000.

17 Pearce, W. B. (2004). The coordinated management of meaning. In W. B. Gudykunst (Ed.), Theorizing about intercultural communication (pp. 35–54). Thousand Oaks, CA: Sage. p. 97

18 Kegan, R. (1982). The evolving self: Problem and process in human development. Cambridge, Mass.: Harvard University Press. p. 100.

19 Pearce (1989). Communication and the human condition. Carbondale: University of Illinois Press, p. 93.

Chapter 3

20 Conversation with Ken and Mary Gergen September 2016.

21 Pearce (1989). Communication and the human condition.carbondale: University of Illinois Press.

Chapter 4

22 Siegel, D., The developing mind: How relationships and the world interact to shape who we are, Guilford Press NY 2012; Parrish-Sprowl, J., & Parrish-Sprowl, S. (2014). Communication complex: An applied elaboration of the communication perspective. Presented at the 3rd annual CMM Learning Exchange, Oracle, AZ: CMM Institute for Personal and Social Evolution.

Chapter 5

23 Daloz, L. A. (1996). Common fire: Leading lives of commitment in a complex world. NY: Beacon Press.

Chapter 6

24 Gergen, K. (2009). An invitation to social construction (2nd ed. ed.). London, England: Sage; Gergen, K. J. (1985). The social constructionist movement in modern psychology. American Psychologist, 40(3), 266-275. doi: http://dx.doi.org/10.1037/0003-066X.40.3.266

25 Davidson, R., Begley, S., (2012). The Emotional life of your brain: How its unique patterns affect the way you think, feel, and live--and how you can change them, Penguin Press.

26 http://philadelphia.cbslocal.com/2016/08/24/woman-chooses-message-of-love-in-response-to-hateful-vandalism-on-her-property/

Chapter 7

27 Pearce, K. & Pearce, B.,
http://www.cmminstitute.net/content/kim-barnett-pearce-evolution-cmm

TAOS INSTITUTE PUBLICATIONS

See all the Taos Publications at
www.taosinstitute.net/taos-books-and-publications

Taos Institute Publications Books in Print

* * * * * * *

Taos Tempo Series:
Collaborative Practices for Changing Times

The Magic of Organizational Life, (2017) by Mette Vinther Larsen

Paths to Positive Aging: Dog Days with a Bone and Other Essays, (2017) by Mary Gergen and Kenneth J. Gergen

70Candles! Women Thriving in Their 8th Decade, (2015) by Jane Giddan and Ellen Cole (also available as an e-book)

U&ME: Communicating in Moments that Matter, New & Revised! (2014) by John Stewart (also available as an e-book)

Relational Leading: Practices for Dialogically Based Collaboration, (2013) by Lone Hersted and Kenneth J. Gergen (also available as an e-book)

Retiring But Not Shy: Feminist Psychologists Create their Post-Careers, (2012) edited by Ellen Cole and Mary Gergen (also available as an e-book)

Developing Relational Leadership: Resources for Developing Reflexive Organizational Practices, (2012) by Carsten Hornstrup, Jesper Loehr-Petersen, Joergen Gjengedal Madsen, Thomas Johansen, Allan Vinther Jensen (also available as an e-book)

Practicing Relational Ethics in Organizations, (2012) by Gitte Haslebo and Maja Loua Haslebo

Healing Conversations Now: Enhance Relationships with Elders and Dying Loved Ones, (2011) by Joan Chadbourne and Tony Silbert

Riding the Current: How to Deal with the Daily Deluge of Data, (2010) by Madelyn Blair

Ordinary Life Therapy: Experiences from a Collaborative Systemic Practice, (2009) by Carina Håkansson

Mapping Dialogue: Essential Tools for Social Change, (2008) by Marianne "Mille" Bojer, Heiko Roehl, Mariane Knuth-Hollesen, and Colleen Magner

Positive Family Dynamics: Appreciative Inquiry Questions to Bring Out the Best in Families, (2008) by Dawn Cooperrider Dole, Jen Hetzel Silbert, Ada Jo Mann, and Diana Whitney

* * * * * * *

Focus Book Series

Communicating Possibilities: Brief Introduction to the Coordinated Management of Meaning (CMM), (2017) by Ilene C. Wasserman & Beth Fisher Yoshida

*A Student's Guide to Clinical Supervision: You are not Alone, (*2014) by Glenn E. Boyd (also available as an e-book)

When Stories Clash: Addressing Conflict with Narrative Mediation, (2013) by Gerald Monk, and John Winslade (also available as an e-book)

Bereavement Support Groups: Breathing Life into Stories of the Dead, (2012) by Lorraine Hedtke (also available as an e-book)

The Appreciative Organization, Revised Edition (2008) by Harlene Anderson, David Cooperrider, Kenneth J. Gergen, Mary Gergen, Sheila McNamee, Jane Watkins, and Diana Whitney

Appreciative Inquiry: A Positive Approach to Building Cooperative Capacity, (2005) by Frank Barrett and Ronald Fry (also available as an e-book)

Dynamic Relationships: Unleashing the Power of Appreciative Inquiry in Daily Living, (2005) by Jacqueline Stavros and Cheri B. Torres

Appreciative Sharing of Knowledge: Leveraging Knowledge Management for Strategic Change, (2004) by Tojo Thatchenkery

Social Construction: Entering the Dialogue, (2004) by Kenneth J. Gergen, and Mary Gergen (also available as an e-book)

Appreciative Leaders: In the Eye of the Beholder, (2001) edited by Marge Schiller, Bea Mah Holland, and Deanna Riley

Experience AI: A Practitioner's Guide to Integrating Appreciative Inquiry and Experiential Learning, (2001) by Miriam Ricketts and Jim Willis

* * * * * * *

Books for Professionals Series

Social Constructionist Perspectives on Group Work, (2015) edited by Emerson F. Rasera

New Horizons in Buddhist Psychology: Relational Buddhism for Collaborative Practitioners, (2010) edited by Maurits G.T. Kwee

Positive Approaches to Peacebuilding: A Resource for Innovators, (2010) edited by Cynthia Sampson, Mohammed Abu-Nimer, Claudia Liebler, and Diana Whitney

Social Construction on the Edge: 'Withness'—Thinking & Embodiment, (2010) by John Shotter

Joined Imagination: Writing and Language in Therapy, (2009) by Peggy Penn

Celebrating the Other: A Dialogic Account of Human Nature, (reprint 2008) by Edward Sampson

Conversational Realities Revisited: Life, Language, Body and World, (2008) by John Shotter

Horizons in Buddhist Psychology: Practice, Research and Theory, (2006) edited by Maurits Kwee, Kenneth J. Gergen, and Fusako Koshikawa

Therapeutic Realities: Collaboration, Oppression and Relational Flow, (2005) by Kenneth J. Gergen

SocioDynamic Counselling: A Practical Guide to Meaning Making, (2004) by R. Vance Peavy

Experiential Exercises in Social Construction – A Fieldbook for Creating Change, (2004) by Robert Cottor, Alan Asher, Judith Levin, and Cindy Weiser

Dialogues About a New Psychology, (2004) by Jan Smedslund

* * * * * * *

WorldShare Books – Free PDF Download

Spirituality, Social Construction and Relational Processes: Essays and Reflections (PDF version 2016) edited by Duane Bidwell.

Therapy as a Hermeneutic and Constructionist Dialogue: Practices of freedom and of deco-construction in the relational, language and meaning games (PDF version 2016) by Gilberto Limon (Translated from Spanish)

Recovered Without Treatment: The Process of Abandoning Crystal Meth Use Without Professional Help (PDF version 2016) by Pavel Nepustil

Introduction to Group Dynamics: Social Construction Approach to Organizational Development and Community Revitalization, (PDF version 2016), by Toshio Sugiman

Recursos psico-sociales para el post-conflicto" (Psico-social resources for post-conflict) (PDF version 2016), Edited by Angela Maria Estrada

Buddha As Therapist: Meditations (PDF version 2015), by G.T. Maurits Kwee

Diálogos para la transformación: experiencias en terapia y Otras intervenciones psicosociales en Iberoamérica – Volumen 1 and 2 (PDF version 2015), by Dora Fried Schnitman, Editora

Education as Social Construction: Contributions to Theory, Research and Practice (PDF version 2015) Editors: Thalia Dragonas, Kenneth J. Gergen, Sheila McNamee, Eleftheria Tseliou

Psychosocial Innovation in Post-War Sri Lanka (PDF version 2015) by Laurie Charles and Gameela Samarasinghe

Social Accountability & Selfhood (PDF version 2015, original publication date – 1984, Basil Blackwell, Inc.) by John Shotter

Construccionismo Social Y Discusion De Paradrigmas En Psicologia: Indeterminacion, Holismo y Juegos de Lenguaje vs. La Teoria Pictorica del Lenguaje (PDF versión 2015) by Roberto Aristequi

{In}Credible Leadership: A Guide for Shared Understanding and Application (PDF version 2015) by Yuzanne Mare, Isabel Meyer, Elonya Niehaus-Coetzee, Johann Roux

Etnia Terapéutica: Integrando Entornos (PDF version 2015) by Jeannette Samper A. and José Antonio Garciandía I.

Post-modern Education & Development (Chinese edition, PDF version 2014) Introduction by Shi-Jiuan Wu (**後現代教育與發展　　介紹吳熙珇**)

Exceeding Expectations: An Anthology of Appreciative Inquiry Stories in Education from Around the World (PDF version 2014) Story Curators: Dawn Dole, Matthew Moehle, and Lindsey Godwin

The Discursive Turn in Social Psychology (PDF version 2014), by Nikos Bozatzis & Thalia Dragonas (Eds.)

Happily Different: Sustainable Educational Change – A Relational Approach (PDF version 2014), by Loek Schoenmakers

Strategising through Organising: The Significance of Relational Sensemaking, (PDF version 2013), by Mette Vinther Larsen

Therapists in Continuous Education: A Collaborative Approach, (PDF version 2013), by Ottar Ness

Contextualizing Care: Relational Engagement with/in Human Service Practices, (PDF version 2013), by Janet Newbury

Nuevos Paradigmas, Cultura y Subjetividad, by Dora Fried Schnitman

Novos Paradigmas Em Mediação (PDF versión 2013, original publicación date 1999), Dora Fried Schnitman y Stephen LittleJohn (editors)

Filo y Sofía En Diálogo: La poesía social de la conversación terapéutica (PDF version 2013, original publicación date 2000), Klaus G. Deissler y Sheila McNamee (editors). Traducción al español: Mario O. Castillo Rangel

Socially Constructing God: Evangelical Discourse on Gender and the Divine (PDF version 2013), by Landon P. Schnabel

Ohana and the Creation of a Therapeutic Community (PDF version 2013), by Celia Studart Quintas

From Nonsense Syllables to Holding Hands: Sixty Years as a Psychologist (PDF version 2013), by Jan Smedslund

Management and Organization: Relational Alternatives to Individualism (PDF version 2013, reprinted with permission) Edited by Dian Marie Hosking, H. Peter Dachler, Kenneth J. Gergen

Appreciative Inquiry to Promote Local Innovations among Farmers Adapting to Climate Change (PDF version 2013) by Shayamal Saha

La terapia Multi–Being. Una prospettiva relazionale in psicoterapia, (PDF version 2013) by Diego Romaioli

Psychotherapy by Karma Transformation: Relational Buddhism and Rational Practice (PDF version 2013) by G.T. Maurits Kwee

La terapia como diálogo hermenéutico y construccionista: Márgenes de libertad y deco-construcción en los juegos relacionales, de lenguaje y de significado (PDF versión 2012) by Gilberto Limón Arce

Wittgenstein in Practice: His Philosophy of Beginnings, and Beginnings, and Beginnings (PDF version 2012) by John Shotter

Social Construction of the Person (PDF version 2012). Editors: Kenneth J. Gergen and Keith M. Davis, Original copyright date: 1985, Springer-Verlag, New York, Inc.

Images of Man (PDF version 2012, original copyright date: 1975) by John Shotter. Methuen, London.

Ethical Ways of Being (PDF version 2012). By Dirk Kotze, Johan Myburg, Johann Roux, and Associates. Original copyright date: 2002, Ethics Alive, Institute for Telling Development, Pretoria, South Africa.

Piemp (PDF version 2012), by Theresa Hulme. Published in Afrikaans.

For book information and ordering, visit Taos Institute
Publications at:
www.taosinstitutepublications.net

For further information, call: 1-888-999-TAOS, 1-440-338-6733
Email: info@taosinstitute.net

CPSIA information can be obtained
at www.ICGtesting.com
Printed in the USA
FFOW03n1746080517
35354FF